amazing places on Britain's coast

Dorset Libraries
Withdrawn Stock

Published by The Reader's Digest Association Limited
London · New York · Sydney · Montreal

The most amazing places on Britain's coast

Contents

Introduction

Wherever you go along Britain's coast you discover amazing places to thrill and fascinate you, from perfect beaches, dizzying cliffs and other wonders of nature to the manufactured genius of castles, piers and lighthouses. Areas of Outstanding Natural Beauty include the 18-mile spit of ever-shifting shingle at Chesil Beach in Dorset and the wild and beautiful Hebridean island of Barra in Scotland. Wonders crafted by people encompass the perfect medieval castle of Beaumaris, guarding the approaches to Anglesey in North Wales, and fanciful follies, such as a water tank disguised as a weatherboarded house at Thorpeness, Suffolk. The coast's industrial heritage can be found in the kipper smokehouses of Craster in Northumberland and the gaunt remains of the once-thriving tin-mining industry on the shores around Chapel Porth in Cornwall.

DIRECTIONS With directions to help you find each entry, this book will allow you make the most of every moment spent by the sea. For places such as nature reserves or historic sites, remember to check on opening times.

The following abbreviations for heritage or conservation organisations are used throughout the book:

EH	English Heritage www.english-heritage.org.uk
NT	National Trust www.nationaltrust.org.uk
LT	Landmark Trust www.landmarktrust.org.uk
Cadw	Welsh Historic Monuments www.cadw.wales.gov.uk
HS	Historic Scotland www.historic-scotland.gov.uk
NTS	National Trust for Scotland www.nts.org.uk
RSPB	Royal Society for the Protection of Birds www.rspb.org.uk

SOUTHWEST

ENGLAND

Cornwall

BEDRUTHAN Among the most dramatic features on the Cornish coast are the massive slate rocks that rise from the beach at Bedruthan Steps. The vast natural monoliths are named after a legendary local giant, who is supposed to have used them as stepping stones.

One, Samaritan Island, is so called after a brig wrecked there in 1846; her cargo of silks and satins was 'rescued' by local people, who used the luxurious materials for dresses and quilts. Another has been christened Queen Bess Rock, but its supposed likeness to the profile of Queen Elizabeth I has been lost through erosion. The best view of the rocks is from the clifftop above the beach. A steep flight of steps leads down to the shore, where an expanse of sand is exposed at low tide.

BOSCASTLE The narrow, winding inlet of Boscastle harbour provides rare shelter for boats on this intimidating stretch of coast. Tourism is the main activity today, but in the 19th century Boscastle was a busy commercial port, importing coal and timber and exporting slate and china clay. Ships had to be towed in by eight-man rowing boats because of the dangerous harbour entrance. A blowhole in the outer harbour sometimes sends out plumes of spray.

BEDRUTHAN ➡ 5 miles N of Newquay off B3276.
BOSCASTLE ➡ 14 miles S of Bude at junction of B3263 and B3266.

A mile-long walk eastwards along the South West Coast Path leads to Pentargon, a small bay where a waterfall cascades 37m (120ft) over black cliffs onto the narrow beach below.

CHAPEL PORTH As you approach Chapel Porth, it appears as a blue wedge of sea between heather-covered

hills. The lane ends in a National Trust car park at the head of a sandy, shingle-backed beach. The rocks flanking it provide many sun traps, but swimmers and surfers should beware of currents and undertows. In a steep valley southeast of the cove, the ruined engine house and chimney of the Charlotte United mine are a reminder of the tin and copper mines that flourished round Chapel Porth in the 19th century.

To the north are the buildings of Wheal Coates tin mine, which was worked from at least the 17th century until its closure in 1889. Dramatically positioned on the edge of a cliff is the Towanroath engine house, constructed in 1872. This housed the pumping engine that was needed to keep the mine free of water.

GLENDURGAN The superb subtropical garden (NT) straddles a valley running down to the Helford River.

Planted at the beginning of the 19th century, the garden includes tulip trees as well as a beautifully planned cherry laurel maze and arrays of azaleas, camellias and hydrangeas.

CHAPEL PORTH ▶ At end of minor road, 2 miles SW of St Agnes.
GLENDURGAN ▶ Just S of Mawnan Smith, 5 miles S of Falmouth.

HELFORD Hugging an inlet on the Helford estuary, the peaceful village has thatched cottages and gardens

that blaze with colour in summer – in spring the nearby woodlands have swathes of daffodils and primroses. In former times, trading ships brought French rum, tobacco and lace from continental Europe and duty was collected at the old custom house. Today, the former port is much quieter. You can take a ferry between the north and south banks of the estuary or explore its many creeks and inlets under your own steam.

KYNANCE COVE Huge outcrops of serpentine rock shelter the popular beauty spot, where the pale golden sands are

completely covered at high tide. The cove is best visited within 2½ hours of low tide, when it is possible to explore the caves to the west. These include the Devil's Bellows, which is transformed into a blowhole by the surging sea. One of the giant mounds of rock on the beach is known as Albert Rock, after a visit in 1846 by Prince Albert and the royal children. Nearby Asparagus Island is so named because wild asparagus used to grow on its slopes.

The South West Coast Path leads southwards past Lion Rock, and slopes down to tiny Caerthillian Cove before rounding Lizard Point. Cornish heath – a species of heather unique to the county – is among the wild flowers that flourish in the Lizard National Nature Reserve. Since 2000, Britain's rarest breeding bird, the Cornish chough, has begun nesting here again after a 50-year gap.

HELFORD ➡ On minor roads, 8 miles E of Helston.
KYNANCE COVE ➡ At end of minor road, 1 mile W from A3083 just N of Lizard.

LIZARD A scattered village on a lonely plateau, Lizard is a centre for fashioning the local serpentine rock into ornaments. The richly coloured, polished stone became very popular in the 19th century, after Queen Victoria visited Cornwall and ordered items for Osborne, her new house on the Isle of Wight.

A lane from the village leads southwards through farmland for half a mile to the tip of the flat-topped Lizard peninsula. The waters that lash this on three sides have caused many shipwrecks. Near the end of the road is a lighthouse dating from 1751. At tiny, rocky Church Cove, to the east of Lizard village, there is just room for a slipway and an old boathouse. The cove was once the site of a pilchard fishery, and fish cellars built around a courtyard beside a stream can still be seen. A footpath south from Church Cove leads past the lifeboat station at Kilcobben Cove to the slopes of Bass Point, with good views of the cliffs.

MEVAGISSEY The heart of Mevagissey is its large harbour where fishing boats and pleasure craft mingle. Attractions include an aquarium, a small museum and the nearby World of Model Railways. Restaurants, bars, pubs and shops line the village's only through street, reflecting its popularity with holidaymakers. This and the steep, narrow side streets are unsuitable for cars – visitors are directed to car parks at the edge of the village.

LIZARD ➡ 10 miles S of Helston on A3083.
MEVAGISSEY ➡ 6 miles S of St Austell on B3273.

To the south of Mevagissey is the former fishing and boat-building village of Portmellon. Seen on a sunny day in summer, the cove has a serene quality, but high tides and strong easterly winds sometimes beat the shore, sending spray into the streets. As a defence against the sea, the houses are protected by stout shutters and fronted by concrete walls 1m (3ft) thick.

About 2 miles northwest of Mevagissey are the Lost Gardens of Heligan, where a long-neglected 19th-century garden has been carefully restored to feature summerhouses, a crystal grotto, rockeries and a jungle-like ravine.

MORWENSTOW A colourful 19th-century churchman, Robert Stephen Hawker, dominates the history of this hamlet.

Hawker was its vicar for 40 years, and achieved some success as a poet. He built the vicarage, whose curious chimneys represent the towers of churches he had known. The wooden hut in which Hawker wrote some of his poems can be reached down 17 steps from the top of the precipitous Vicarage Cliff.

The Norman Church of St Morwenna, notable for its stone carvings and 16th-century carved bench ends, is dedicated to a 9th-century Celtic saint. More than 40 seamen are buried in the churchyard, and the figurehead of the *Caledonia*, wrecked in September 1843, is a memorial to some of them. The land between the church and the cliffs is National Trust property.

MORWENSTOW ➡ 7 miles N of Bude off A39.

MOUSEHOLE Dylan Thomas described this little port as 'the loveliest village in England'. Houses crowd around a harbour with curving stone quays, where a small area of sand is revealed at low tide. Mousehole was a major pilchard port until nearby Newlyn developed in the 19th century. One local fishwife, Dolly Pentreath who died in 1777, was thought to be the last woman to speak Cornish as her native tongue. Nowadays, pleasure craft and fishing boats use the harbour, and shark and deep-sea fishing trips start there.

Steep Raginnis Hill, south of the harbour, leads up to the Wild Bird Hospital and Sanctuary, which is open to visitors. Raginnis Hill is also the starting point for an exhilarating 2 mile walk to Lamorna.

PADSTOW Put on the map by TV chef Rick Stein and his seafood restaurant, this popular holiday resort retains the character of a working fishing port. The 15th-century Church of St Petroc stands amid Padstow's network of narrow streets, which converge on the harbour, a pleasing clutter of boats, lobster pots and ropes. The town was well known to Elizabethan sea captains – Sir Walter Raleigh spent much of his time there when he was Warden of Cornwall in the late 16th century. It was a thriving commercial port in the 19th century, but the Doom Bar sandbank at the mouth of the Camel River prevented the passage of larger modern vessels.

MOUSEHOLE ➡ 3 miles S of Penzance off B3315.
PADSTOW ➡ 8 miles W of Wadebridge on A389.

The harbour is now the embarkation point for fishing trips and pleasure cruises. The port's history is illustrated in a little museum above the library; the Shipwreck Museum on South Quay displays items recovered from wrecks around the Cornish coast. Also on the quayside are the tanks of the National Lobster Hatchery where visitors can learn about marine conservation and the local fishing industry.

The town is at its most traditional during the May Day festival, when a figure in black tarpaulin and a grotesque mask, dubbed the 'Obby 'Oss, is paraded through the streets. Dancers and musicians follow in its wake until the festival reaches its climax when the 'Obby 'Oss is ritually 'done to death'.

POLPERRO Picturesque narrow streets lined with whitewashed cottages lead down to a little harbour, which swarms with holidaymakers in summer. Non-resident traffic is banned in the fishing village of Polperro, but visitors can ride in a shuttle minibus or a horse-drawn carriage from the car park to the harbour. To the west of the harbour, a climb of some 40 steps leads to Chapel Hill, with wide-ranging views. A 2 mile clifftop walk heads east from Polperro's Heritage Centre to Talland Bay.

POLPERRO ➡ 4 miles W of Looe on A387.

POLZEATH Surfers and other holidaymakers flock to the village of Polzeath and the vast, flat sands of Hayle Bay. The coast path north of Polzeath leads to the cliffs and farmland of the Pentire peninsula and Rumps Point (NT), where there are traces of the banks and ditches of an Iron Age fort. South of Polzeath at Trebetherick is the long sandy beach

of Daymer Bay, with views across the Camel estuary to Stepper Point. The simple Church of St Enodoc, surrounded by a golf course, is the burial place of the poet Sir John Betjeman, who loved Cornwall, often celebrating it in verse. The church was almost completely buried by sand in the 19th century, but it was restored in the 1860s and is now used for regular worship.

POLZEATH ➡➤ 5 miles N of Wadebridge off B3314.

PORTHCURNO The tiny triangle of Porthcurno's beach, made up of ground-down shells, was once known as the 'centre of the universe'. The cove was the landing place for undersea cables that linked Britain to the world telegraph network. The first cable was laid in 1870.

The open-air Minack Theatre – an amphitheatre cut into the high cliffs just south of the cove – stages performances in summer. A mile-long walk along the coast path eastwards from Porthcurno leads to the headland of Treryn Dinas, where an earth-and-stone rampart is all that remains of one of Cornwall's most substantial Iron Age promontory forts. Nearby Logan Rock is a huge granite boulder. It once balanced in such a way that it could be made to rock, or 'log', but in the 1820s a group of high-spirited sailors dislodged the stone and were unable to restore it.

PORT ISAAC One of the few working fishing villages left on the north Cornwall coast, Port Isaac is best approached on foot from a car park above the village. Fish is sold in the cellars beside a small, 18m (60ft) wide slipway, and there are a number of seafood restaurants. Boat trips starting from the harbour offer a chance to go fishing for mackerel and cod or just sightseeing. Flower-filled hanging baskets decorate cottages in the village's maze of narrow alleys, which include Squeeze-ee-belly Alley – perhaps a warning about the dangers of consuming too many cream-ladened Cornish delicacies.

PORTHCURNO ➡ 3 miles SE of Land's End off B3315.
PORT ISAAC ➡ 8 miles N of Wadebridge via B3314 and B3267.

PRAA SANDS A mile-long crescent of sand is enclosed by two headlands and high dunes. The western end of the beach is sheltered from westerly winds by the cliffs of Hoe Point. The coast path leads eastwards towards rugged Lesceave Cliff (NT). Gaze over the bay and you may spot terns, auks and gannets, and passing dolphins or porpoises.

ST IVES The town has been an artists' colony since the 1880s, attracting talents as diverse as James McNeill Whistler, Patrick Heron and Walter Sickert. Trewyn Studio, where the sculptor Dame Barbara Hepworth used to work until her death in 1975, is now a memorial museum to her. Among some 30 art galleries, Tate St Ives, on a hillside above the surfing beach of Porthmeor, displays the work of 20th-century painters and sculptors, and offers wide views of the Atlantic.

Fishermen still use the harbour, and visitors can arrange their own fishing trips from the quayside. An unusual and attractive way to approach St Ives is to park at Lelant and go by train. The train ride offers spectacular views of the coast, including Porthminster's golden beach.

ST JUST IN ROSELAND Subtropical plants, including Chilean myrtle and Chinese fan palms, tumble down to the waterside in the churchyard of the 13th-century Church of St

PRAA SANDS ▶ Just S of A394, 6 miles W of Helston.
ST IVES ▶ 12 miles NE of Penzance via A30 and A3074.
ST JUST IN ROSELAND ▶ 2 miles N of St Mawes off A3078.

Just. The hamlet's evocative name comes from the Cornish word *ros*, or *roos*, meaning promontory. Most of the land around the coastal path south to St Mawes is owned by the National Trust.

ST MAWES Set on steep slopes at the end of a peninsula flanked by Carrick Roads and the Percuil River,

St Mawes clusters around a harbour busy with fishing boats and pleasure craft, where in summer many day visitors arrive by the ferry from Falmouth. St Mawes Castle (EH) was built in the mid 16th century to a clover-leaf design of three bastions around a low tower. It faces Falmouth's Pendennis Castle on the opposite side of Carrick Roads, and its grounds provide a splendid vantage point from which to watch big ships ease into the waterway. Nearby are the Lamorran House Gardens, where subtropical plants and water gardens cover precipitous hillsides. The gardens open two days a week from spring to early autumn.

ST MICHAEL'S MOUNT The massive granite crag bears a spectacular battlemented castle,

built in the 14th century on the site of an earlier monastic shrine. Rising from the waters facing Marazion, the island is now in the care of the National Trust, and much of the castle is open to the public. At low tide a causeway joins the island with Marazion; small boats provide a link with the mainland when the causeway is covered.

ST MAWES ▪▸ 18 miles S of Truro at end of A3078.
ST MICHAEL'S MOUNT ▪▸ Off Marazion (A394): on foot via causeway at low tide or ferry (not winter) at high tide.

TINTAGEL Arthurian myth envelops Tintagel, which fully exploits the legends popularised by Lord Tennyson. His mid 19th-century *Idylls of the King* made much of the village's supposed links with King Arthur and his Knights of the Round Table. Nothing, though, can take away from the awesome impact of the reputed site of Arthur's court, The Island – actually a craggy headland connected to the shore by a strip of wave-lashed sand and shingle.

TREBAH Planted in a ravine by the Quaker polymath Charles Fox, a 10ha (25 acre) garden slopes steeply to a private sandy beach. Palms and 100-year-old tree ferns flourish, along with exotic water plants, giant Brazilian rhubarb and towering rhododendrons. One path zigzags through a rare and beautiful collection of Mediterranean plants.

TRELISSICK Encompassing rolling parkland, landscaped gardens with subtropical shrubs and woodland plantations, the estate of Trelissick (NT) is bounded on three sides by the River Fal and two of its many creeks. The 18th-century mansion is open to visitors on a few days each year. Five miles of paths include a riverside woodland walk that passes the embarkation point for the King Harry Ferry, a car ferry pulled across the Fal by a diesel-powered chain drive.

TINTAGEL ➡ Signposted off B3263 between Boscastle and Trewarmett.
TREBAH ➡ Just S of Mawnan Smith, 5 miles S of Falmouth.
TRELISSICK ➡ 6 miles S of Truro, off B3289 King Harry Ferry road.

The reputed site of King Arthur's court

Devon

BRAUNTON BURROWS

A wilderness of sand dunes, some 30m (100ft) high, spreads out behind Saunton Sands. The southern part is a national nature reserve with some 400 species of flowering plant. These include purple thyme and yellow bird's-foot, as well as the rarer sand pansy and sand toadflax. The dunes are occasionally used for military training; at such times access is restricted.

BURGH ISLAND

Perched on low cliffs, the resort of Burgh Island offers wide views over a sandy beach curling round to the mouth of the Avon. The island is joined to the mainland by sand at low tide; at other times, it can be reached by sea tractor. The 14th-century Pilchard Inn was once a smugglers' haunt, while the Burgh Island Hotel makes a stylish retreat for the wealthy. At low tide, walkers can follow a 4-mile 'tidal lane', marked by a line of poles, from the nearby village of Bigbury to Aveton Gifford along the west bank of the Avon.

CLOVELLY

Donkeys and sledges are the only form of transport in Clovelly's steep, cobbled main street, flanked by whitewashed cottages. A small harbour at the foot of the street

BRAUNTON BURROWS ➤ SW of Braunton, at junction of A361 and B3231, 8 miles W of Barnstaple.
BURGH ISLAND ➤ Foot crossing at low tide from Bigbury-on-Sea, end of B3392, off A379, 6 miles NW of Kingsbridge.

was built in Tudor times. It was the base of a fishing fleet, which prospered in the 18th and 19th centuries on huge catches of herring. Now boats take visitors on trips around the bay.

If time seems to have stood still in Clovelly, it is mainly due to Christine Hamlyn, who owned the village from 1884 to 1936 and devoted her life to protecting its buildings and beauty. Descendants of the Hamlyn family live at Clovelly Court. The house is not open to the public, but the gardens can be visited.

The most attractive way to approach Clovelly is along the 3-mile wooded toll road known as the Hobby Drive, which leaves the A39 at Hobby Lodge. Cars must be left in the car park outside the village. In summer, a Land Rover ferries visitors between the top of the village and the harbour, avoiding the main street. At The Milky Way Adventure theme park, 1½ miles to the south, visitors can see birds of prey and falconry displays, as well as farm animals.

CROYDE A stream runs through the heart of Croyde, past thatched cottages and shops selling clotted cream. The small, sandy bay is a magnet for surfers. The National Trust car park at the northern end of Croyde Bay is the start of a mile-long clifftop walk to Baggy Point, where gulls, fulmars, shags and kestrels breed. Baggy Erratic, under the low cliff at Baggy Point, is a 50-tonne boulder carried by glaciers from western Scotland during the last Ice Age.

CLOVELLY ➍ On B3237, 2 miles N of A39 between Bude and Bideford.
CROYDE ➍ 12 miles W of Barnstaple via A361 and B3231.

DAWLISH WARREN Langstone Rock, a huge block of sandstone with a wave-carved arch, dominates the view to the south of Dawlish Warren. This 1½-mile sandspit, jutting across the mouth of the Exe estuary, is a popular holiday resort, complete with a funfair (reached by a lane under the railway line) and a long sandy beach abounding with shells. Swimmers should beware of the dangerous fast-flowing currents that circulate off the tip of the spit. If you enjoy

birdwatching, Dawlish Warren National Nature Reserve embraces an extensive area of mudflats and salt marsh, as well as dunes and sandy shore. These attract large numbers of waders and wildfowl, including dunlins, black-tailed godwits and Brent geese.

Among hundreds of flowering plants growing in the reserve is the Warren crocus, whose delicate lilac-blue flowers can be seen nowhere else in mainland Britain.

DAWLISH WARREN ➨ 10 miles S of Exeter off A379.

HARTLAND QUAY Dark jagged cliffs slide into the sea at Hartland Quay, whose small harbour was built in the late 16th century. Intended as a safe haven on this hazardous stretch of coast, the harbour was almost destroyed by storms in the 19th century. Nowadays, there is a museum devoted to seafaring history and local wrecks. Go at low tide and you may see some of the vessels that came to grief.

The road to Hartland Quay passes through the hamlet of Stoke, where the 14th-century St Nectan's Church has a 40m (130ft) tower, built as a landmark for sailors. In the churchyard is Strangers Hill, where some of the victims of local shipwrecks were buried.

Nearby Hartland Abbey stands on the site of a monastery founded in the 12th century. During the Dissolution of the Monasteries in the 16th century, Henry VIII gave it to William Abbot, the Sergeant of his Wine Cellar. The house, which is open to the public in summer, was extensively rebuilt in the 18th century. A woodland walk leads through the grounds to the coast.

LYNTON & LYNMOUTH High cliffs and narrow valleys resembling mountain passes led the Victorians to call the area round Lynton and Lynmouth 'Little Switzerland'. In August 1952, Lynmouth suffered a disastrous flood that swept away trees, buildings and bridges and claimed 34 lives.

HARTLAND QUAY ➡ Off A39, 18 miles W of Bideford via Hartland village.
LYNTON & LYNMOUTH ➡ 18 miles W of Minehead on A39 Barnstaple road.

Boat trips can be taken from Lynmouth harbour, dominated by its so-called Rhenish Tower. Originally built in the 19th century to supply a local home with seawater for baths, the tower was destroyed during the 1952 flood but later reconstructed. From Lynmouth, a road with a one-in-four gradient leads up to Lynton, standing on a plateau 152m (500ft) above the harbour. Alternatively, visitors can use a two-car cliff railway, which opened in 1890. The two cars each have a counterbalancing water tank filled at the top of the hill and emptied at the foot.

Lynton's delightful Lyn and Exmoor Museum, housed in a restored 17th-century cottage, has exhibitions of local history and arts and crafts. It contains a range of oddities, from an otter trap and a peat plough to a homemade barometer and a 100-year-old jar of gooseberries. You can take woodland walks from nearby Hollerday Hill or trek up a path to the Valley of Rocks.

MORTEHOE

MORTEHOE A Norman barrel roof and fine Tudor bench ends are features of Mortehoe's 13th-century St Mary Magdalene Church. The village, perched on a hill on the edge of Woolacombe, is the starting point for walks over the headland to Morte Point. From there, 2 miles of coast path lead northeast round Rockham Bay, where steps descend to a sandy beach, and on to Bull Point lighthouse.

MORTEHOE ➡ On minor roads, 4 miles W of Ilfracombe.

SALCOMBE With one of the West Country's finest natural harbours, Salcombe is a long-established haven for yachtsmen. The town's narrow streets are packed with visitors in summer, when the estuary becomes a forest of masts and billowing sails. A maritime museum illustrates Salcombe's history as a sailing port and a US base during the Second World War. Hire a small boat and you can explore the estuary as far inland as Kingsbridge.

SLAPTON SANDS A granite monument at Slapton Sands records the US Army's gratitude to the local people. In the Second World War, US troops used the beach to rehearse for the D-Day landings. But tragedy struck during one ill-fated exercise in April 1944, when 638 servicemen died after German E-boats sank two of their landing craft and a further 308 were killed on the beach by 'friendly' fire. The shallow lake of Slapton Ley and its neighbouring reed beds are a nature reserve, the haunt in winter of huge flocks of migrating wildfowl.

VALLEY OF ROCKS Pinnacles of sandstone flank the 1½ mile long, riverless Valley of Rocks, east of Lee Bay. Topping the main ridge that separates the valley from the sea is the rock formation called Rugged Jack. Wild goats graze on the cliffs, where seabirds such as guillemots and razorbills nest.

SALCOMBE ■→ 7 miles S of Kingsbridge on A381.
SLAPTON SANDS ■→ 8 miles E of Kingsbridge on A379.
VALLEY OF ROCKS ■→ 1 mile W of Lynton on minor roads.

SOUTHWEST ENGLAND

Dorset

ABBOTSBURY Honey-coloured houses line the streets of this attractive village, once the domain of the nearby Abbey of St Peter. A wall and archway of the abbey still remain, as does an impressive stone tithe barn, built in about 1400 to store the monastic wealth. A lagoon behind the shingle beach is another reminder of those times. The abbey monks farmed swans here for special feasts. Nowadays, the Swannery gives sanctuary to hundreds of mute swans, which breed in the lagoon.

In St Nicholas's Church, take a careful look at the pulpit. It is still pockmarked with shots fired during the Civil War, when Abbotsbury fell to Cromwell's Parliamentarians. Then climb to the 14th-century St Catherine's Chapel (EH) crowning a hill overlooking the village. You will be rewarded with superb views across Chesil Beach to the great sweep of Lyme Bay.

In a sheltered valley just west of the village, you can wander through the subtropical Abbotsbury Gardens, where an exceptionally mild microclimate allows exotic trees and shrubs to flourish outdoors all year round.

BROWNSEA ISLAND The patchwork of woods, grassland and heath that covers Brownsea Island (NT) is home to a surprising variety of wildlife. This is the last southern refuge of

ABBOTSBURY ▶▶ 6 miles NW of Weymouth on B3157 Bridport road.
BROWNSEA ISLAND ▶▶ In Poole Harbour, ferries from Poole and Sandbanks.

the red squirrel, and there is a large heronry in the northern half of the island – a nature reserve. Exotic imports include sika deer and semi-wild peacocks. Lord Baden-Powell held the first Scout camp on Brownsea in 1907. You can reach the island by ferry from Poole Quay and Sandbanks.

CHESIL BEACH The great pebble strand of Chesil Beach slices along the coast for 18 miles from West Bay in the northwest to Portland in the southeast, its pebbles naturally graded from fine gravel at the West Bay end to large cobbles at Portland. East of Abbotsbury, the beach rises to a height of 12m (40ft) and protects a lagoon called the Fleet – a nature reserve that attracts swans, waders such as curlew and dunlin, and many wintering wildfowl. This part of the beach can be reached from either end of the reserve, at Abbotsbury or Portland. To protect breeding birds from being disturbed, there is no pedestrian access between May and August.

DURDLE DOOR The spectacular natural arch of Durdle Door, carved by the sea through a limestone headland, is flanked on either side by shingle coves. Both coves, reached by steep tracks down the cliffside, are popular with swimmers and subaqua divers. At Bat's Head, farther west, the waves have gouged out another, smaller hole in the rock.

CHESIL BEACH ➡ 1 mile W of B3157, between Portland and Abbotsbury.
DURDLE DOOR ➡ 8 miles SW of Wareham, just W of Lulworth Cove at end of B3070.

GOLDEN CAP Soaring to 189m (620ft) above sea level, the golden-orange sandstone summit of Golden Cap is the tallest cliff in southern England. Dramatic views from the top stretch as far as Portland Bill to the east and Start Point to the west. The cliff is part of a National Trust estate that embraces most of the coastal land between Charmouth and Seatown. It includes 18 miles of walks over terrain ranging from steep cliffs to undulating meadows and clumps of ancient woodland. You can take a number of different paths to reach the top of Golden Cap, but the shortest route is from the car park at Langdon Hill. Stonebarrow Hill, to the west, has a car park and information centre.

HENGISTBURY HEAD Heath, woods, meadow and marsh cover Hengistbury Head, a narrow, hooked finger of land that almost completely encloses Christchurch Harbour. From the 36m (118ft) summit of Warren Hill – an important archaeological site, with traces of Stone Age settlement – enjoy superb views across the Solent to the Isle of Wight. Double Dykes is another reminder of the past – two defensive ditches built in Viking times. Children will enjoy the 'land train', a mock railway from Double Dykes to Mudeford Sandbank, a strip of dunes at the Head's tip. Alternatively, there is a ferry to the sandbank from Mudeford Quay on the other side of the harbour. The Head is an important wildlife conservation area.

GOLDEN CAP ➡ 1 mile S of A35 Bridport–Lyme Regis road at Chideock.
HENGISTBURY HEAD ➡ 5 miles E of Bournemouth.

KIMMERIDGE BAY An oil well is an unlikely sight on the Dorset coast, yet the 'nodding donkey' pump that bobs on the unstable cliff at Kimmeridge produces about 4.5 million litres (1 million gallons) of oil a year. A tower, visible across the bay, was built in about 1820 by an amateur astronomer, the Rev. John Clavell. His family home, Smedmore House, dates from the 1630s and is open a few days each year. At the east end of the bay is Purbeck Marine Wildlife Reserve, where visitors can wander along natural ledges to explore marine wildlife.

LULWORTH COVE High cliffs of crumbling chalk form a natural amphitheatre round this beautiful, oyster-shaped bay, while to its west lies Stair Hole, a similar cove in the making. Lulworth Heritage Centre explains the area's geology.

Running east from Lulworth Cove, a narrow road leads across a Royal Armoured Corps tank and gunnery range to the village of East Lulworth. Although the range is generally closed to the public during the week, it is open most weekends and on weekdays in certain holiday periods. The picnic area on Povington Hill has fine views, and several waymarked footpaths, including the South West Coast Path, cross the range.

Lulworth Castle, standing in parkland on the edge of East Lulworth, was designed as a hunting lodge in the 17th century. The 30m (100ft) towers at its four corners are another place for superb views across the surrounding countryside.

KIMMERIDGE BAY ➡ 4 miles SW of Corfe Castle, off minor road from Corfe to Lulworth.
LULWORTH COVE ➡ 5 miles S of Wool, via B3071 and B3070.

SOUTHWEST ENGLAND Dorset

LYME REGIS **A dashing past involving smugglers and a Civil War siege** lies behind Lyme's present existence as a charming resort. Many of these adventures centred on The Cobb, the 183m (600ft) stone breakwater protecting the harbour. This remains the town's focal point, with visitors enjoying its marine aquarium and the salty atmosphere of yachts and fishing boats. Narrow streets lined with colour-washed houses climb from the seafront, and there are several vantage points with fine views of Black Ven, the fossil-bearing cliffs east of Lyme. There are samples of local fossils at the award-winning Philpot Museum and the Dinosaurland Fossil Museum.

If the scene seems familiar when you visit, don't be surprised – Lyme has featured in many a novel and film. In Jane Austen's *Persuasion*, the boisterous Louisa Musgrove is concussed when she falls on some steps on The Cobb. A cloaked Meryl Streep stands forlorn on the wave-lashed Cobb in the 1981 film of *The French Lieutenant's Woman*, based on John Fowles' novel. Fowles lived in Lyme for more than 35 years at Belmont House, a Georgian villa, now belonging to the Landmark Trust.

A path from Holmbush car park at the top of Pound Street leads west to the Undercliffs National Nature Reserve. Here, in 1839, some 8ha (20 acres) of chalkland tumbled seawards in a massive landslide, creating what became known locally as Goat Island. The footpath through the reserve is rough and slippery in wet weather, but it is possible to walk for a couple of miles to enjoy the peace of this unspoiled corner of southern England.

LYME REGIS ▶ 15 miles SE of Honiton.

Somerset

BURNHAM-ON-SEA A wooden lighthouse rises
improbably on stilts from the sandy beach at Burnham.
At the start of the 19th century, the enterprising Rev. David
Davies sank wells on the shore in an attempt to create a spa
town. The spa was not a success, but the venture established
Burnham as a seaside resort. Another suprise lies behind
the long promenade, inside the 14th-century Church of
St Andrew. The carved figures of cherubs and angels once
belonged in the chapel of London's Whitehall Palace. They
were brought to Burnham in 1820.

DUNSTER At one end the turrets of Dunster Castle
and at the other the 17th-century Yarn Market dominate
Dunster's broad high street lined with medieval buildings.
The castle, on a steep hill with terraces of magnolias, fuchsias
and rhododendrons, was remodelled in 1870, but it still has
plasterwork and an oak staircase from the 17th century. Two
gateways and part of the walls that surrounded the original
village of Dunster still stand, along with a 12th-century
church, priory and gardens; nearby are an old tithe barn and
monks' dovecote. By the river, and near the medieval Gallox
Bridge, is a 17th-century watermill.

BURNHAM-ON-SEA ➠ 10 miles S of Weston-super-Mare.
DUNSTER ➠ 2 miles E of Minehead on A396.

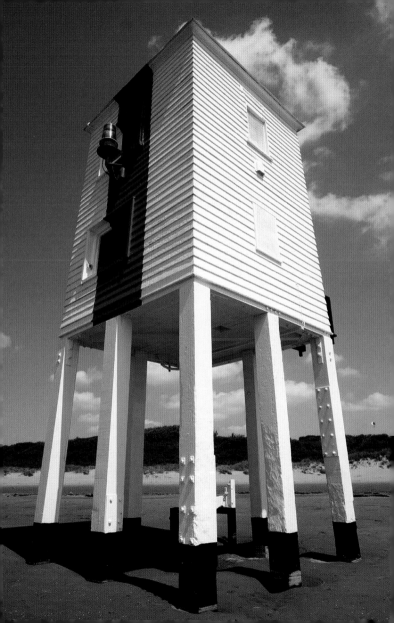

Channel Islands

HERM The scenery on this compact island, 1½ miles long and half a mile wide, includes towering cliffs, wooded valleys, sandy beaches and enough pastureland to support a small herd of Guernsey cows. Herm, which is leased from the States of Guernsey, lies a 20-minute boat trip from St Peter Port on Guernsey. There is a 15th-century granite-built Manor House, and by the small harbour are a few pastel-coloured cottages, a hotel, a pub and a shopping square. There are no cars or roads.

North of the harbour, a path cuts across heathland from sandy Fishermans Beach and Bears Beach to the island's showpiece, Shell Beach. Millions of tiny shells have been washed up on this golden strand, some from as far away as the Gulf of Mexico. About 10 minutes' walk away is Belvoir Bay, small and secluded. Then the going gets tough as the path climbs along the cliffs and valleys of Herm's southern half. Another walk leads to the tiny St Tugual Chapel, which dates from Norman times.

MONT ORGUEIL CASTLE The magnificent 13th-century keep, Elizabethan tower and rambling outworks of Mont Orgueil Castle overlook the harbour at Gorey on Jersey's east

HERM ➡ Daily ferries in summer (reduced service in winter) from St Peter Port, Guernsey.
MONT ORGUEIL CASTLE ➡ 4 miles E of St Helier.

coast. Other local attractions include Royal Bay of Grouville, a sandy beach to the south of Gorey, which sweeps down to La Rocque Point, the winter home of large numbers of migrating waders, including turnstones and sanderlings.

SARK The island of Sark is still run along feudal lines, under a seigneur whose feudal rights date back to 1565,
when they were granted by Queen Elizabeth I. No cars are allowed on the island. Instead, tractor-drawn trailers take visitors up the steep hill from the harbour. Horse-drawn carriages can also be hired for drives around Sark, and bicycles are available.

The island is about 3 miles long and 1½ miles across, and at the southern end it is almost cut in two by La Coupée, a natural causeway of rock, 76m (250ft) above sea level. The southern section is called Little Sark.

Many of Sark's bays are beautiful, but the views from its headlands are the island's real glory. From Havre Gosselin, on the west coast, the panorama extends across to the lonely, privately owned Brecqhou Island. At the foot of the cliffs, the sea licks around jagged rocks and probes the dark depths of the Gouliot Caves. On the northeastern shore, the view from the Banquette Point stretches as far as the lighthouse at Point Robert to the south and, on a clear day, the coast of Normandy in France, some 20 miles away.

SARK ➽ Ferries: all year from St Peter Port, Guernsey;
Apr–Sept from St Helier, Jersey.

SOUTH

ENGLAND

Hampshire

BUCKLERS HARD Two rows of 18th-century cottages and a grassy 'high street' sloping down to the Beaulieu River make up this beautifully restored village. It was a busy shipbuilding centre, and two warships for Nelson's fleet were built here – *Agamemnon* in 1781, and *Euryalus* in 1803. At low tide, the stumps of the cradles for these ships are still visible. The Maritime Museum has tableaux re-creating 18th-century life. There are river cruises, and a riverside walk to Beaulieu.

HURST CASTLE Built by Henry VIII in the 1530s and 40s, Hurst Castle (EH) crouches at the end of a lonely spit. You can reach it by a strenuous 2 mile walk across a pebble causeway from just outside Milford, or by ferry in summer from Keyhaven. The castle has a 12-sided central tower and two Victorian 38 ton guns; an exhibition relates the castle's history.

NEEDS ORE POINT A haven for birdwatchers, part of the North Solent National Nature Reserve lies along Beaulieu River's shoreline. It includes Gull Island and has the country's largest population of black–headed gulls. Entry is by permit from Beaulieu estate office, at the National Motor Museum.

BUCKLERS HARD ▶ 7 miles E of Lymington off B3054 Beaulieu road.
HURST CASTLE ▶ 3 miles S of Lymington off A337.
NEEDS ORE POINT ▶ Access is along a private gravel road, signposted Warren Lane; it begins 2 miles south of Bucklers Hard.

PORTCHESTER CASTLE The castle's ancient outer
walls are those of Europe's most complete surviving Roman
fortress. The Norman keep of Portchester Castle (EH) houses
an exhibition of its history, and a path from the Water Gate leads
to the shore and offers good views of Portsmouth Harbour. A
coastal path close by heads west towards Fareham.

The chalk escarpment of Portsdown Hill, 1 mile northeast
of Portchester, has footpaths and outstanding views across
Portsmouth. Fort Nelson, built by Lord Palmerston in the 1860s,
houses the Royal Armouries Museum of Artillery.

PORTCHESTER CASTLE ▓➜ 6 miles N of Portsmouth off A27
Fareham road.

PORTSMOUTH DOCKS A fortress town since the 15th century, Portsmouth is England's most important naval base.

In the 1490s, when ships purpose-built for war became too large to repair on the beach, the world's first dry dock was created here and in 1540 Henry VIII founded the Royal Dockyard here.

Among the dockyard's Georgian storehouses is the Royal Naval Museum, together with Henry VIII's warship *Mary Rose* and Lord Nelson's flagship, HMS *Victory*. The *Mary Rose* Museum displays the objects found on the ship, remarkably well preserved by the silt. These include cast-bronze guns with Henry's coat of arms and the only surviving Tudor longbows. The ship itself has been withdrawn from public view until 2012 when it will be on show in a new boat-shaped museum. You can board HMS *Warrior*, which was the world's most advanced warship when it was launched in 1860, and is docked in the harbour. The *Warrior*'s trump card was its iron hull and the central armour-plated box, which protected its machinery.

Soaring above the retail and entertainment complex at Gunwharf Quays is the 170m (558ft) Spinnaker Tower, which offers spectacular views along the coast.

In Gosport, a short boat trip across the harbour, is the Royal Navy Submarine Museum, where two subs are on view, *Holland I* and HMS *Alliance*. *Holland I*, Britain's first practical operational submarine, was launched in 1901 but scrapped in 1913 when it became outdated. HMS *Alliance* remained in service from 1947 until 1973 and is preserved fully equipped.

PORTSMOUTH DOCKS ▪▶ Portsmouth Historic Dockyard, W of the city centre with access through Victory Gate at the corner of Queen Street and The Hard. Royal Navy Submarine Museum, S of Gosport town centre over Haslar Bridge (foot ferry from Portsmouth).

HMS *Victory*

Isle of Wight

COWES Regattas take place at East Cowes every summer, making the most of the long promenade, which allows superb views of yacht racing outside the harbour. A chain ferry across the River Medina links the town to the world sailing centre of West Cowes, where yachts ride at anchor in the bay below the headquarters of the Royal Yacht Squadron. A maritime museum is housed in the town's library. You can cross to Southampton by ferry from East Cowes or by passenger hydrofoil from West Cowes.

FRESHWATER BAY Two chalk stacks, smaller versions of The Needles, stand in the bay here, and another is being carved out of the cliff face by the relentless sea. Badly eroded chalk cliffs rise beside a curving sea wall and a steeply shelving pebble beach. Farringford House, on the western edge of Freshwater, was the home of the poet Lord Tennyson between 1853 and 1864; it is now a hotel.

OSBORNE HOUSE Queen Victoria's country retreat, Osborne House (EH) provides an intimate glimpse of the monarch's family life, as it has been left almost unchanged

COWES ➡ On N coast of island, ferry from Southampton.
FRESHWATER BAY ➡ 2 miles S of Totland on A3055.
OSBORNE HOUSE ➡ 1 mile SE of East Cowes off A3021.

since her death there in 1901. The Queen and her husband, Prince Albert, commissioned the architect Thomas Cubitt to build the palace in 1845. It stands in magnificent Italianate gardens with views across the Solent.

A grove of cork trees in nearby Barton Manor Gardens and Vineyards was planted by Prince Albert. He also designed the flamboyantly Gothic Church of St Mildred at Whippingham, a mile to the southwest.

THE NEEDLES The three towering 30m (100ft) pinnacles are the remnants of a chalk ridge that used to join the Isle of Wight to the mainland. A pleasure park with funfair amusements and picnic areas stands on The Needles peninsula near a vast parking area. From here a walk of almost a mile across the headland leads you past the Old Battery (NT), a restored Victorian fort, to a closer, even more spectacular view of The Needles. A small exhibition relates how First World War firing trials made the chalk cliffs unstable, forcing the battery's relocation further from the edge.

Tranquillity can be found east of the peninsula on the grassy chalk ridge of Tennyson Down, named after the poet Lord Tennyson, who lived at nearby Farringford House. He walked on the down regularly, and declared the air there to be worth 'sixpence a pint'. A monument to him was erected on the summit in 1897.

THE NEEDLES ➠ 4 miles SW of Yarmouth at end of B3322.

SOUTH ENGLAND

Kent

BROADSTAIRS There are reminders of Charles Dickens at almost every corner of the narrow, twisting streets of the sedate town of Broadstairs, where the novelist spent many summer holidays. Now a private house, the battlemented Bleak House is where Dickens wrote *David Copperfield*. A house on the seafront was once the home of Miss Mary Strong, the model for the character Betsey Trotwood in the book; it is now the Dickens House Museum. In June each year, Broadstairs holds a week-long Dickens Festival, when people dress up in Dickensian costume.

Viking Bay has a sandy beach, sheltered by the curving pier, where fishing boats land their catch.

CHATHAM In 1547, when Henry VIII first maintained a storehouse to service his fleet at anchor in the River Medway, the town's long history as a naval dockyard began. Drake, Hawkins and Nelson sailed from Chatham, and Nelson's flagship HMS *Victory* was one of 400 ships built there. The working dockyard closed down in 1984, but the site has been given a new lease of life as The Historic Dockyard museum.

Among the many 18th and early 19th-century buildings in the dockyard is the Ropery, where you can watch ropes being

BROADSTAIRS ➡ 18 miles NE of Canterbury.
CHATHAM ➡ 30 miles SE of London, access from M2.

made. The Wooden Walls gallery re-creates a day in 1758, and demonstrates how craftsmen built the warship HMS *Valiant* in the age of sail, while outside on the dockyard you can explore the decks and cabins aboard a Victorian naval sloop, a Second World War destroyer and a Cold War submarine.

Cruises along the Medway can be taken on the paddle steamer *Kingswear Castle*, based at the dockyard, while Dickens World, beside the Medway, has themed attractions based on life in the 19th century. Fort Amherst was built in its present form to defend the naval dockyard from attack by Napoleon's armies and has more than a mile of tunnels.

DEAL In the days of sail, naval fleets and merchantmen anchored in The Downs

– the stretch of water between Deal and the treacherous Goodwin Sands – waiting for favourable winds to help them on their journey. That era is recalled by the Timeball Tower, whose time-keeping mechanism was used by sailors in The Downs to check their chronometers. The tower now houses a museum, while the Deal Museum explores the town's maritime history. A quiet town with a steeply sloping shingle beach, Deal remains much as it was in the 18th century. In the west of the town is the Tides Leisure Pool complex.

Deal Castle (EH) was built by Henry VIII in the shape of a Tudor rose, and a roadside plaque just south of the castle makes the doubtful claim that Julius Caesar first landed here in 55 BC.

DEAL ⭢ 8 miles N of Dover on A258.

DOVER The town's naval significance dates back through many centuries: the Romans made Dover the headquarters of their northern fleet; in the Middle Ages Dover was one of the Cinque Ports; and during both World Wars it was shelled and bombed from across the English Channel. Today, cross-Channel ferries and cargo ships come and go from the giant harbour.

On a hill above the eastern side of the town is the huge fortress of Dover Castle (EH). The castle's square keep was started in the 1180s; outer walls were added and remodelled in later centuries, and a labyrinth of tunnels was dug in Napoleonic times. During the Second World War some of the tunnels were used as an operations centre, where the evacuation of troops from Dunkirk was planned, and others were adapted as a hospital. Guided tours of the tunnels are available.

On a grassy mound next to the castle are the 12m (40ft) high remains of a Roman *pharos*, or lighthouse, built soon after the Romans arrived in the 1st century AD, and beside which stands the Saxon Church of St Mary-in-Castro. In a clearing behind the castle, the granite outline of an aircraft sunk into the turf commemorates Louis Blériot, who landed there after making the first cross-Channel flight in 1909.

The town's museum, housed in the Dover Discovery Centre, tells the story of Dover since prehistoric times and has the Bronze Age Boat, the world's oldest known seagoing vessel. Nearby are the remains of a Roman town house with wall paintings and a hypocaust (heating system).

DOVER ■▶ 80 miles SE of London on A2.

In the Middle Ages Dover
was one of the Cinque Ports

DUNGENESS The windswept shingle promontory,
where thick fog can roll in suddenly, and whose coastline
is forever changing, has been a constant danger to shipping.
Two lighthouses stand on the foreshore: graceful Dungeness
lighthouse, which throws a beam for 17 miles, and the tall, brick
tower of the disused 1904 lighthouse. The latter has spectacular
coastal views from its parapet. The base of Samuel Wyatt's
lighthouse of 1792 has been converted into houses and flats.

Behind the lighthouses loom the massive square blocks of
Dungeness nuclear power station. The late film director Derek
Jarman created a wild garden in its shadow which is still there
today. Dungeness is also the southern terminus of the Romney,
Hythe and Dymchurch Railway, whose miniature steam trains
puff along the coast to Hythe, nearly 14 miles away.

Dungeness RSPB Reserve, off the Lydd–Dungeness road,
has an information centre and waymarked walk. The reserve
is a wintering ground for migratory birds, and more than
300 species have been recorded here, including firecrests, little
terns and stone curlews.

ELMLEY MARSHES Owned by the RSPB, wigeon, teal
and white-fronted geese winter on the marshes, while
breeding birds include redshanks, lapwings and shovelers.
The reserve is reached by a 2 mile track, a mile north of the
Kingsferry Bridge and Sheppey Crossing.

DUNGENESS ➡ 5 miles S of New Romney on minor roads.
ELMLEY MARSHES ➡ On Isle of Sheppey, 6 miles SE of
Sheerness.

RECULVER Sharply etched against the sky, the twin towers of Reculver's ruined St Mary's Church are the main landmark along the 10 mile stretch of coast between Herne Bay and Margate. The grassy area round the towers is the site of the Roman fortress of Regulbium, built in the 3rd century AD to guard the northern end of the Wantsum Channel, which once separated the Isle of Thanet from the mainland of Kent. In AD 669, King Egbert of Kent founded a monastery and church inside the fort; the towers on the site today date from a rebuilding in the 12th century.

Most of the church was demolished in the 19th century, but the towers were regarded as such an important navigational aid that they were restored by Trinity House. Alexanders, a plant with sprays of yellow flowers, grows here; it was introduced by the Romans, who ate the celery-flavoured stems.

THE WARREN A wilderness of cliffs, scrub, grassland and woodland, The Warren is a favourite place for walkers, who follow a waymarked trail that starts at the Martello tower visitor centre. More than 200 species of bird have been recorded here; chaffinches and yellowhammers may be seen all year, and migrating birds such as blackcaps, chiffchaffs and nightingales arrive in spring and autumn. The hummocky land beneath the chalk cliffs has been created by landslips. A major slip, in 1915, buried the railway line that crosses The Warren.

RECULVER ➡ 3 miles E of Herne Bay on minor roads.
THE WARREN ➡ Access from Martello tower visitor centre,
1 mile NE of Folkestone town centre.

WHITSTABLE With its rows of weatherboarded
fishermen's cottages, black-tarred boat sheds and sailing
dinghies, Whitstable has a strong flavour of the sea. The busy
harbour, once the port for Canterbury, has an active fishing
fleet, and it is lined with sheds where you can buy fresh fish.
For centuries Whitstable was famous for the quality of its
oysters, and although the oyster trade gradually declined due
to changes in climate and sea conditions, in the 1960s it was
revived and began to flourish again. At the far end of the
harbour, the Oyster Fishery Exhibition tells the story of the
industry, and Whitstable-grown oysters can be sampled there.
In July the town holds an oyster festival.

Smuggling in spirits and tobacco was once rife along
the Kent coast and the town's narrow passageways, such as
Squeeze Gut Alley, provided convenient escape routes for
both smugglers and local children playing cat-and-mouse
with the police. Whitstable Castle was built by a London
businessman as a seaside residence in the 1790s and today is
the site of the annual May Day celebrations; its pretty gardens
are open to the public.

The quiet resort of Tankerton is separated from Whitstable
by a tree-covered hill topped by a ship's mast and a pair of
cannons. A wide grass bank slopes down from the village to
the beach, from which a shingle finger, known as The Street,
protrudes. It is dangerous to swim near The Street, but at low
tide it is a favourite place for shell collectors.

WHITSTABLE ➠ 8 miles N of Canterbury.

Sussex

BEACHY HEAD The Normans called it Beau Chef, meaning 'Beautiful Headland', but over the centuries the name of this colossal chalk rampart has been corrupted to 'Beachy'. The 163m (535ft) cliff rises sheer from the rocky foreshore, and from its grassy summit the view on a clear day takes in the English Channel from Dungeness in the east to the Isle of Wight in the west and the red-and-white lighthouse far below. Exhibits in the Beachy Head Countryside Centre include a rock pool with tides.

BOSHAM One of the south coast's most renowned beauty spots, the harbour village of Bosham, pronounced 'Bozzam', sits on a small wedge of land between two tidal creeks. Its sailing club is housed in an old quayside watermill in the marina, while Quay Meadow (NT) is a grassy picnic area, beyond which rises the steeple of the Saxon Holy Trinity Church.

BRIGHTON The onion-domed Royal Pavilion forms an extraordinary centrepiece to the queen of British seaside resorts. Brighton's oriental fantasy, its interior as whimsical as its exterior, was the early 19th-century creation of the Prince

BEACHY HEAD ➡ 2 miles SW of Eastbourne off A259.
BOSHAM ➡ 3 miles W of Chichester off A259.
BRIGHTON ➡ 60 miles S of London.

Regent, who later became George IV. Fashionable society followed the prince to Brighton, and the town expanded steadily, its elegant terraces and squares surrounding the old fishing village of Brighthelmstone. Brighton Museum and Art Gallery, housed in the former stables of the Royal Pavilion, traces the town's development into a major resort.

The narrow streets of the old village are now a pedestrianised shopping area known as The Lanes, which has many antiques, clothes and jewellery shops, while the pebbly beach leads down to a strip of sand at low-tide. The Palace Pier, renowned for its amusements and funfair, looks out over the old West Pier, which is awaiting restoration. Volk's Electric Railway, which rattles along the seafront, was the first such railway in Britain when Magnus Volk opened it in 1883. The Sea Life Centre and the Fishing Museum are also on the seafront.

CAMBER SANDS The vast dunes that loom over Camber have been replanted with marram grass and shrubs to prevent erosion. Fenced footpaths lead across the dunes to Camber Sands, where the sea goes out for half a mile at low tide. The coast road from Rye zigzags past gravel pits and across golf links; walkers should take care, as there is a danger of being cut off by fast, incoming tides. East of Camber, the dunes gradually give way to the shingle of Dungeness, where the currents become progressively more dangerous.

CAMBER SANDS ➡ 3 miles SE of Rye on minor roads.

CUCKMERE HAVEN At a gap in the chalk cliffs, 18th-century smugglers found an ideal place to land cargoes of brandy, lace and other French contraband. The tranquil River Cuckmere, whose name is pronounced 'Cookmere', makes a series of enormous loops through water meadows before reaching Cuckmere Haven. The main road is a mile inland, and the stone-scattered beach is reached only by footpath along the valley. There is a large car park near the start of the walk, at Exceat, pronounced 'Ex-seet'.

The eastern side of the Cuckmere Valley and the western end of the Seven Sisters cliffs make up a country park that includes meadows, downland, chalk cliffs, salt marsh and shingle. Barns by the Seaford to Eastbourne road at Exceat house a visitor centre and The Living World exhibition, where you can see stick insects, scorpions, butterflies and a seashore-life display.

DE LA WARR PAVILION The long, low lines and great sweeps of glass of the De La Warr Pavilion dominate the quiet resort of Bexhill. It was designed by Erich Mendelsohn and Serge Chermayeff, winners of an architectural competition inspired by the Mayor of Bexhill, the 9th Earl de La Warr, to promote the town. The building was built in 1935 and embodies many of the key features of Modernism. It was the first major building in Britain to be constructed around a framework of welded steel. The building was extensively restored in 2005 as an arts venue.

CUCKMERE HAVEN ➨ Access on foot from Exceat on A259, 6 miles W of Eastbourne.
DE LA WARR PAVILION ➨ On seafront, Marina (B2182), Bexhill.

EASTBOURNE A lively pier and a turquoise-roofed bandstand, where military bands play in summer, stand at the centre of 3 miles of seafront in Eastbourne, which has plenty of stuccoed Victorian buildings. Colourful public gardens that line the seafront include the Carpet Gardens, where flowerbeds are laid out in the patterns of Persian carpets. The beach is mainly shingle, with sand at low tide; fishing trips are available, and boat trips take visitors past Beachy Head and the Seven Sisters cliffs. On the seafront is Wish Tower, a restored Martello tower, while the neighbouring Lifeboat Museum is housed in a former lifeboat station. Eastbourne's heritage centre, a few minutes' walk inland, traces the town's growth since the 17th century, and the nearby How We Lived Then museum of shops illustrates how people shopped and lived from 1850 to 1950. Further east along the seafront is The Redoubt, a restored Napoleonic fortress housing military exhibitions.

Polegate Windmill, on Eastbourne's northern outskirts, is a restored tower mill built in 1817 and open to the public on various summer days and Bank Holidays. Between Eastbourne and Pevensey Bay is Sovereign Harbour, a large marina and leisure area.

PAGHAM HARBOUR Now a nature reserve, dunlins, grey plovers, curlews and Brent geese are among the many species that gather on the mudflats of this former port, while

---

EASTBOURNE ▶ 20 miles E of Brighton.
PAGHAM HARBOUR ▶ 5 miles S of Chichester on B2145.

much of the surrounding land is a haven for small mammals, insects and butterflies. The reserve is reached along a path from a visitor centre at Sidlesham, 2 miles north of Selsey.

The village of Pagham is centred on the seafront, and the mainly 13th-century Church of St Thomas à Becket is one of the few indications that an earlier settlement existed. Pagham's sandy beach, backed by pebbles, has a car park and cafés.

RYE This gem of a medieval hilltop town is entered through an imposing stone gateway; its narrow streets, many of them cobbled, rise to the fine Norman Church of St Mary, distinctive for its 'quarterboys', gilded cherubs that strike the bells on the tower clock. Rye is surrounded by water on three sides: the Rother to the east; the Tillingham to the west; and the Royal Military Canal to the south. It has a small fishing fleet, and there are usually fishing boats moored in the Rother.

Lamb House (NT), built in the 18th century, was the home of the American novelist Henry James from 1897 to 1914, while steep, cobbled Mermaid Street, with its half-timbered Mermaid Inn, was once a haunt of smugglers. The 13th-century Ypres Tower, all that remains of Rye Castle, has a museum with exhibits that include one of the world's oldest fire engines; the tower overlooks the Gun Garden, where cannon still point out to sea. Rye Heritage Centre, on Strand Quay, houses the Town Model, showing Rye as it was in the late 19th century.

RYE ➡ 11 miles NE of Hastings on A259.

SEAFORD HEAD NATURE RESERVE Behind the 86m (282ft) cliffs of Seaford Head is a nature reserve

where migrant birds, including willow warblers, chiffchaffs, whitethroats and redstarts, stop to feed while heading south in autumn. Ring ouzels and pied flycatchers may also be seen, and nightingales are heard in spring. A clifftop path from Seaford to the headland gives spectacular views along the coast, while the path from the car park to Hope Gap gives a splendid view of the scalloped white wall of cliff known as the Seven Sisters.

SEVEN SISTERS Between Cuckmere Haven and Birling Gap, the striking vertical chalk cliffs rise and fall like the waves

in the sea far below. Despite its name, there are in fact eight summits in the range, the highest of which is 77m (253ft).

WINCHELSEA Weatherboarded cottages and tile-hung houses face each other across streets laid out on a grid

pattern in this sleepy little town. Winchelsea now stands more than a mile inland, but during the Middle Ages it was one of the principal harbours on the south coast until the build-up of shingle gradually cut it off from the sea. Winchelsea was attacked by the French, who destroyed most of the Church of St Thomas the Martyr; only the choir and side chapels remain intact. Three medieval gateways survive, as does the Court Hall.

SEAFORD HEAD NATURE RESERVE ➠ S of Seaford on minor road off A259.
SEVEN SISTERS ➠ 6 miles W of Eastbourne off A259 Brighton road.
WINCHELSEA ➠ 2 miles S of Rye on A259.

EAST

ANGLIA

Essex

MALDON One of the oldest recorded settlements in Essex,
Maldon has ancient seafaring traditions that live on at The Hythe, with restored Thames barges looming over the quayside. The quay itelf leads onto a promenade, where a sweep of sloping grass gives you good views of pleasure craft thronging the River Blackwater. The high street rises from the harbour to the Church of All Saints, with its triangular tower, and to the 15th-century Moot Hall, which can be visited on Saturday afternoons in summer.

The 13m (43ft) *Maldon Embroidery*, created in 1991 to mark the 1,000th anniversary of the Battle of Maldon, is displayed in the Maeldune Heritage Centre, which was formerly St Peter's Church. The Plume Library on the first floor of the building contains some 6,000 antiquarian books. In the grounds of the church, of which only a tower remains, the Millennium Garden has an array of plants used in the 10th century for medicinal and culinary purposes.

NORTHEY ISLAND Surrounded by creeks and marshes, and screened by mature hedgerows,
Northey Island (NT) resembles a secret garden. You can reach the secluded spot along a private road through South House Farm and over a

MALDON ➡ 12 miles E of Chelmsford on A414.
NORTHEY ISLAND ➡ S of Maldon, off minor road towards Mundon, or walk along sea wall from The Hythe, Maldon. Access to island by permit from Warden.

causeway that is covered at high tide; you will need a warden's permit to visit the island, which is part farm, part nature reserve. A nature trail leads over fields to a hide from where herons, shelducks, pintails and curlews can be seen.

Stone Age flint scrapers have been found here, and the causeway is probably Roman. In AD 991, an army of Danes crossed the causeway to defeat the Saxons, the story of which is recounted in the epic poem, *The Battle of Maldon*.

ST OSYTH The village is named after the daughter of a 7th-century East Anglian king, beheaded by Danish invaders,
because she would not worship their idols. The Priory (now a private house) was built in her honour. There are weatherboarded houses in the well-preserved centre. To the west lies Howlands Marsh Nature Reserve, a low-lying area grazed by sheep.

ST PETER'S CHAPEL One of Britain's oldest churches is set on an isolated spot on the site of the Roman fortress
of Othona. St Cedd – a Northumbrian missionary to the East Anglians who arrived here in AD 653 – used stones from the fortress to build the chapel, whose full name is St Peter's-on-the-Wall. It stands on open grassland, and the last half mile has to be walked from Bradwell-on-Sea. Footpaths lead along the sea wall in both directions.

ST OSYTH ▶ 4 miles W of Clacton-on-Sea on B1027.
ST PETER'S CHAPEL ▶ Signposted from Bradwell-on-Sea, off B1021, 8 miles N of Burnham-on-Crouch.

SOUTHEND-ON-SEA Originally a village at the 'south end' of medieval Prittlewell Priory, Southend developed

as a seaside resort in the early 19th century and boomed during Victorian times, spreading to embrace surrounding villages. Southend's pier – at 1.3 miles the longest pleasure pier in the world – has regained some of its former glory after fires in 1976 and 2005. An electric railway runs alongside the walkway, and the pier museum is open in summer. A tree-lined esplanade with a Victorian bandstand overlooks the resort's sand and shingle beach, which becomes muddy towards low-water mark.

Seafront entertainments include the Adventure Island fairground and an aquarium, where visitors can walk underwater through a glass tunnel and enter a shark exhibition through a model of the jaws of a great white shark. Among the town's annual events is a race to Greenwich contested by 20 or so magnificent sailing barges.

TILBURY FORT Built in 1682, Tilbury Fort (EH) was meant to defend the Thames against the Dutch and the French. A

moat surrounds it on the inland side, and on the river side is an elaborate triumphal arch; displays inside show how London was defended against attack from the sea. Tilbury can be reached from Gravesend by a passenger ferry across the Thames; from the ferry terminus a 10-minute walk takes you to the fort.

SOUTHEND-ON-SEA PIER ➡ Southend seafront.
TILBURY FORT ➡ On A1089, 20 miles E of London.

Southend's pier is the longest
pleasure pier in the world

Norfolk

BLAKENEY POINT A lonely shingle spit stretches northwest for about 4 miles from Cley Eye to Blakeney Point, forming the centrepiece of Blakeney National Nature Reserve. Most visitors reach the point by boat from Blakeney or Morston; there is also a footpath from Cley. Blakeney Point is home to nesting colonies of terns, ringed plovers and shelduck, and common and grey seals can often be seen from the boats. Plants on the marshes and dunes on the point's landward side include sea lavender and prickly sea-wort.

BRANCASTER STAITHE A small harbour – a 'staithe' is a bank or landing stage in Old English – stands on a channel almost choked with sand and mud. Small boats take visitors to the national nature reserve of Scolt Head Island, when tides and breeding patterns permit.

   Brancaster Staithe has been known for its shellfish since Roman times; some 250 tonnes of oysters and mussels grown from imported seed are now gathered each year in the creek. Brancaster Staithe merges into Burnham Deepdale, one of the villages in the area jointly known as the 'Seven Burnhams'. Its Church of St Mary has a Norman font carved with a series of 12 illustrations depicting the countryman's working year.

BLAKENEY POINT ➼ Off A149 between Wells-next-the-Sea and Sheringham.
BRANCASTER STAITHE ➼ 7 miles W of Wells-next-the-Sea.

BURNHAM OVERY STAITHE Black-tarred cottages overlook a creek filled with small boats and flanked by a huge area of salt marsh. A mile-long path along the eastern sea wall leads to a boardwalk across dunes to sands, and in summer a ferry runs to Scolt Head Island. To the west of the village, a six-storey tower windmill and a watermill are in view from the A149.

CAISTER-ON-SEA Built in around AD 125 to handle trade between Norfolk and Germany, Caister was once a thriving port. The Roman town (EH) is an excavated part of the port that includes a defensive wall and the south gateway. In the village, a lifeboat memorial lists the nine crew who lost their lives during a rescue operation in 1901. A window in Holy Trinity Church has an inscription of a crewman's remark to King Edward VII: 'Caister men never turn back, Sir.'

CASTLE RISING The quiet hamlet is dominated by the ruins of a Norman fortress, which was once one of the most important fortifications in East Anglia. The ruins of Castle Rising Castle (EH) rest on massive defensive earthworks reached by a bridge over a dry moat. The 15m (50ft) walls of the 12th-century keep remain standing. There are fine views of the surrounding countryside from the ramparts.

BURNHAM OVERY STAITHE ➡ 4 miles W of Wells-next-the-Sea.
CAISTER-ON-SEA ➡ 3 miles N of Great Yarmouth off A149.
CASTLE RISING ➡ 4 miles NE of King's Lynn off A149.

CROMER The self-styled 'gem of the Norfolk coast', popular as a resort since the end of the 18th century, stands on a low, crumbling cliff facing the North Sea. The long sandy beach, which turns to shingle at East Runton Gap, a mile to the west, is reached by a slipway from the promenade. The long pier, built in 1900, has a tranquil air and a large theatre, which hosts a classic seaside variety show in high season. Old flint cottages and winding streets surround the 14th-century Church of St Peter and St Paul, a grand structure even by Norfolk standards, with towers soaring to 49m (160ft). Behind the church, several cottages have been restored to create a museum that evokes the changing character of the town over the past 100 years.

Cromer is known for two things apart from its beach: the quality of its crabs and the brave deeds of its lifeboatmen. The most famous of all lifeboatmen is Henry Blogg, who was coxswain for the Cromer lifeboat from 1909 to 1947; during his years of service, he along with his crew saved 873 people. At the end of Cromer's promenade, the RNLI Henry Blogg Museum illustrates the history of Cromer lifeboats and Blogg's most famous rescues. The centrepiece is Blogg's Watson class lifeboat *H.F. Bailey* from the Second World War.

Cromer lies at the eastern end of the Norfolk Coast Path to Hunstanton, and at the northern end of the Weavers' Way footpath, which travels inland through the Broads to Great Yarmouth, 56 miles to the southeast.

CROMER ➥ 23 miles N of Norwich on A140.

SCOLT HEAD ISLAND NATIONAL NATURE RESERVE

Inaccessibility has contributed to the preservation of wildlife on this island reserve, which comprises continually changing sand dunes, salt marsh, intertidal sand and mudflats and shingle. Colonies of common, Sandwich, arctic and little terns breed in a ternery at the western end, and it is an important breeding ground for ringed plovers, oystercatchers, black-headed gulls and waders. Visitors are not allowed on the reserve between mid April and mid August.

WELLS-NEXT-THE-SEA

The old port has three distinctive parts – the quayside, the old streets behind it and the beach area a mile to the north. The quay has cafés, shops and amusement arcades, while narrow streets lead up to The Buttlands, a tree-shaded green surrounded by dignified Georgian houses.

The sandy beach is almost a mile deep at low tide, and can be reached by road, on foot along the sea wall or from Holkham Gap, or by miniature railway. On reclaimed marshland behind the sea wall, there is a boating lake, while to the east are the largely inaccessible salt marshes that form part of the Holkham National Nature Reserve.

On the Stiffkey road is the terminus of the Wells & Walsingham Light Railway, whose narrow-gauge steam trains run for 4 miles inland as far as the town of Little Walsingham.

SCOLT HEAD ISLAND NATIONAL NATURE RESERVE ➡ A149
Hunstanton to Wells-next-the-Sea road.
WELLS-NEXT-THE-SEA ➡ 21 miles W of Cromer on A149.
WINTERTON-ON-SEA ➡ 7 miles N of Great Yarmouth.

WINTERTON-ON-SEA Norfolk is noted for its soaring church towers, and the 40m (131ft) tower of Holy Trinity and All Saints is one of the finest, dominating the countryside for miles around. Built between 1415 and 1430, the tower remains a landmark for sailors, and Fisherman's Corner inside the church pays tribute to those who have died at sea, with a cross made of items from ships. A road leads northeast from the village to a desert of sand and shingle.

North of the beach are the high, grassy sands of Winterton Dunes National Nature Reserve, where adders, rare natterjack toads and many species of bird, including reed and sedge warblers, whitethroats and chiffchaffs, can be found. A colony of grey seals can regularly be seen down on the shore. A car park at Winterton Beach provides access to the reserve.

Suffolk

ALDEBURGH A main street of Georgian houses and older cottages, behind a wide shingle beach, gives elegance to this small historic town.

Mentioned in the Domesday Book, Aldeburgh was a prosperous port and fishing centre by 1600. Early in the 19th century, it became a popular resort, and in 1948 the composer Benjamin Britten and the singer Peter Pears established the annual music festival, now held at nearby Snape Maltings. The shingle beach stretches north to Thorpeness.

The half-timbered Tudor Moot Hall, or Town Hall, is now almost on the shore, the three roads that originally separated it from the sea having been washed away over the centuries. The Moot Hall is open to visitors in summer and has a museum of local life. Britten and Pears are buried side by side in the churchyard of the largely 16th-century St Peter and St Paul. Inside the church is a bust of the poet George Crabbe, who was born in Aldeburgh in 1754. Britten used Crabbe's pen-portrait of fisherman Peter Grimes in the poem 'The Borough' as the basis of his first opera.

South of the town is a sea wall, which is wide enough for cars to park on, while at Slaughden Quay boats can be launched into the River Alde. A shingle tip called Orford Ness is owned by the National Trust. There is no public right of way along the shoreline, but it can be reached by ferry from Orford.

ALDEBURGH ➠ 28 miles NE of Ipswich on A1094.

DUNWICH Hidden in bushes near a shallow cliff is a
fragment of a 1790 grave – the final link with All Saints'
Church, which collapsed into the sea in about 1920. Saxon and
Norman Dunwich flourished as a port, but in 1286, a huge
storm threw tons of sand and shingle across the harbour mouth,
diverting the River Blyth northwards. Trade was destroyed
and Dunwich declined. By 1677, the sea had reached the
market place, and the town became an estate village. Behind its
Victorian Church of St James are the remains of a leper chapel,
and nearby are the clifftop ruins of a 13th-century friary. The
village museum chronicles the area's history from Roman times.

Two miles south of Dunwich, a stretch of heathland
crowns the crumbling clifftops, from which a waymarked
walk provides panoramic views.

HAVERGATE ISLAND Britain's oldest and largest
breeding colony of avocets returned to breed here in 1947
after an absence of 100 years. This RSPB bird sanctuary is
a marshy island, lying in the long Ore channel that runs
downstream from Orford to the sea. The water levels in the
muddy lagoons are artificially maintained to provide the
correct depth of water for the avocets. Gulls, terns, redshanks
and shelduck are also present. The island can be reached only
by boat from Orford Quay, and you need to request a permit
in advance from the warden.

DUNWICH ➽ 9 miles S of Southwold on B1125.
HAVERGATE ISLAND ➽ By boat from Orford Quay. Book in advance.

IKEN Once a thriving fishing village, Iken is now a scattered hamlet set on high ground above the marshes of the Alde. Good views of the river can be had from the thatched Church of St Botolph, reached through a gate at the end of a narrow cul-de-sac. At Ikencliff, a mile to the west, is a picnic site with views across the reeds and mudflats. Birdlife includes shelducks, redshanks and herons.

ORFORD NESS A prosperous port in the 12th century, Orford was cut off from the sea by the gradual growth of Orford Ness, a spit of shingle measuring some 10 miles. The village's past importance is symbolised by the imposing St Bartholomew's Church, parts of which date from Norman times, and by its 12th-century castle keep (EH). Waymarked paths include an hour's circular walk that starts at the quay. You can also take boat trips up the River Alde or across to Havergate Island RSPB Reserve and Orford Ness.

OULTON BROAD The southern gateway to the Broads, reed-fringed Oulton Broad is one of the finest yachting lakes in Britain, and the only place on the Broads where powerboat race meetings are held. Other attractions include Nicholas Everitt Park on its south bank, the Lowestoft Museum and Mutford Lock, starting point for boat tours along the Waveney to Beccles.

IKEN ▶ 7 miles W of Aldeburgh on minor roads off B1069.
ORFORD NESS ▶ By ferry from Orford Quay, on B1084 N of Woodbridge (A12).
OULTON BROAD ▶ 2 miles W of Lowestoft.

PIN MILL The name Pin Mill is said to be derived from the wooden pegs or 'pins' that were made there and used in boat-bulding. This riverside beauty spot lies at the end of a narrow lane from Chelmondiston. High spring tides on the Orwell allow sailors to moor close to the walls of the Butt and Oyster Inn and order drinks without stepping ashore. The Pin Mill Barge Match, a dazzling display of ornately painted barges, is held annually in late June or early July.

The Cliff Plantation (NT), reached only from a short footpath east of Pin Mill, is an attractive area of pine woodland and open heath stretching along the bank of the river.

SOUTHWOLD A small town that has remained remarkably unchanged for the past century, Southwold is a jewel of the Suffolk coast. Its red-brick and flint cottages and colour-washed houses are built around a series of delightful greens, created after a fire devastated the town in 1659. The promenade is lined with 250 brightly coloured beach huts. The tallest buildings in Southwold are the brilliant white Victorian lighthouse and the great flint Church of St Edmund. The church contains a particularly fine gessowork screen.

Several houses display a Dutch influence, including the little town museum, which is crammed with local memorabilia, photographs, models, wildlife exhibits and fossils. The Sailors' Reading Room on the cliff and the

PIN MILL ➡ Signposted in Chelmondiston on B1456 Ipswich-Shotley Gate road.
SOUTHWOLD ➡ 20 miles S of Lowestoft on A1095.

Lifeboat Museum at the harbour both have mementos of tall ships and oil-skinned heroes, while six 18-pounder cannons stand sentinel on Gun Hill.

You can walk across the common, part of which is a golf course, to Southwold harbour, where you can buy fresh fish from fishermen's huts. From the harbour there is an iron footbridge, and a small passenger ferry in summer across the Blyth to Walberswick. Boat trips up the river are available in summer.

THORPENESS A track leads from the main street to the distinctive House in the Clouds, originally a water tower served by the nearby windmill, but now a private house. The restored windmill, first built at Aldringham 2 miles to the northwest in 1804 and moved to Thorpeness in the 1920s, is open to visitors in summer.

Thorpness is a unique holiday village, centred on a shallow man-made lake called The Meare, on which small boats can be hired. It was created by a local landowner Glencairn Stuart Ogilvie, who inherited the family estate in the early 1900s. The houses vary in style and include Tudor, Jacobean and traditional 18th-century East Anglian tarred weatherboard. Shingle beaches stretch to the north and to the south, where North Warren RSPB Reserve is made up of woodland, heath and wet meadows, which attract swans, geese and ducks in winter.

THORPENESS ▶ 2 miles N of Aldeburgh.

The Tide Mill is today in full working order

WOODBRIDGE Sailmaking, rope-making and boat-building

made Woodbridge prosperous between the 14th and 15th centuries. It is now one of the most attractive towns in East Anglia, with timber-framed and Georgian houses, and steep streets running down to the quayside. Dominating the centre of the triangular market place are the magnificent 15th-century Church of St Mary and the Dutch-gabled Shire Hall, built in the 16th century by Thomas Seckford, a wealthy courtier of Queen Elizabeth I. The hall contains the Suffolk Horse Museum, which illustrates the history of the world's oldest breed of working horse. Nearby Buttrum's Mill is a restored six-storey tower mill built in 1835. Four pairs of original millstones are on display. On the quayside, amid boatyards, chandleries and yachts, is the white, weather-boarded Tide Mill. Built in the 1790s and operating until 1957, the Tide Mill is today in full working order.

Sutton Hoo, east of the town, is a group of grassy burial mounds on a heath where a Saxon king's treasure was excavated in 1939. The site is managed by the National Trust; an exhibition tells the story of early English history. Woodbridge Museum has an exhibition of archaeological findings from Sutton Hoo.

South of Woodbridge is Kyson Hill (NT), a finger of land projecting into the Deben, with panoramic views across the river. A footpath leads you to the muddy foreshore and follows the river bank northwards to Woodbridge quay a mile away.

WOODBRIDGE ➡ 8 miles NE of Ipswich on A12.

NORTHWEST

ENGLAND

Cumbria

CARTMEL Dwarfing the village is the cathedral-like Priory Church of St Mary and St Michael, part of an Augustinian establishment founded in the 12th century. It has a huge east window and an ornately carved tomb built to commemorate the first Lord Harrington, who died in 1347, and his wife; he is thought to have built the south choir aisle of the church. The 14th-century priory gatehouse flanks Cartmel's central square.

ISLE OF WALNEY The 12-mile strip of land provides the shelter that makes Barrow such a fine harbour. A wide expanse of water, dotted with rocks and islets, offers moorings for pleasure craft on the island's landward side, while on the seaward side is a long sandy beach. The North Walney National Nature Reserve is an area of dunes and grassland where birds, such as redshanks and stonechats, congregate; the natterjack toad is also found here. The island's southern end has one of Europe's busiest colonies of lesser black-backed and herring gulls.

PIEL ISLAND & ROA ISLAND Built in the 16th century by the monks of Furness Abbey, Piel Castle (EH) played an important role in Barrow's defences from the 12th century

CARTMEL ➍ 2 miles NW of Grange-over-Sands.
ISLE OF WALNEY ➍ S on minor roads from Barrow-in-Furness.
PIEL ISLAND & ROA ISLAND ➍ Roa Island, off A5087, S of Barrow-in-Furness. Boat from Roa to Piel Island.

and parts of the massive keep and walls survive. Set midway between Roa Island on the mainland and the southern tip of the Isle of Walney, Piel Island can be reached by ferry from Roa Island or, with care, on foot at low tide from South Walney.

The narrow finger of land southeast of Roa Island is occupied by Foulney Island Nature Reserve, reached along a 1½-mile shingle causeway, flooded at high tide. It attracts birds such as terns, eider ducks and dunlin.

RAVENGLASS Narrow-gauge steam-hauled trains head northeast for 7 miles through unspoiled scenery from this village, the terminus of the Ravenglass and Eskdale Railway. A museum in the station tells the story of the line, built in 1875 to carry iron ore to the coast. Ravenglass was the site of the Roman naval base of Glannaventa. The ruins of its bathhouse lie a few minutes' walk from the village.

SANDSCALE HAWS NATURE RESERVE Three miles northwest of Dalton is the Sandscale Haws Nature Reserve (NT), where the rare natterjack toad breeds in spring. In summer, drifts of marsh orchids turn the damp hollows, known as slacks, pink and purple, while rest harrow and dune pansy cover the sand. Walks along the shore give superb views of Black Combe and other fells of the southern Lake District.

RAVENGLASS ▶ 18 miles S of Whitehaven on A595.
SANDSCALE HAWS NATURE RESERVE ▶ Duddon estuary, off A590, W of Dalton-in-Furness.

ST BEES An Irish princess called St Bega established a nunnery here around AD 650. Destroyed by the Vikings, it was refounded as a Benedictine priory in 1120. Nearby is St Bees School, founded in 1583 by Edmund Grindal, Archbishop of Canterbury, and looming over the long sandy beach is St Bees Head cliff.

The RSPB reserve on the headland has one of the largest seabird colonies on England's west coast and is the only breeding ground in England for black guillemots.

ST BEES ➡ 4 miles S of Whitehaven on B5345.

St Bees

WHITEHAVEN

Laid out in the 17th century on a grid pattern and retaining a Georgian elegance, Whitehaven was Britain's first post-medieval planned town. The docks and harbour, built in the 18th and 19th centuries, are used today by fishing boats, pleasure craft and coasters. The Whitehaven Beacon, a museum by the harbour, tells the stories of the town's sailors, miners, slave traders and tobacco merchants. Exhibits include a superb enamel goblet made in 1763. Whitehaven is also the western end of the 140-mile C2C cycle route.

WHITEHAVEN ➨ 14 miles SW of Cockermouth on A595.

Isle of Man

CALF OF MAN The Isle of Man's southwestern tip overlooks the treacherous, rock-strewn passage of Calf Sound. To the south is the massive cliff of Spanish Head and straight ahead are the islets of Kitterland. Behind the islets is the uninhabited island known as Calf of Man.

The island is a nature reserve supporting large colonies of guillemots, razorbills, kittiwakes and puffins; you can also see smaller groups of hooded crows and choughs. In settled weather, boat trips run to the island from Port Erin or Port St Mary.

CASTLETOWN The town's narrow twisting streets seem to huddle for protection round the medieval fortress of Castle Rushen. Castletown was the island's capital until 1874, and a building now occupied by the local authority councillors was once used for meetings of the House of Keys – the elected lower house of Tynwald, the Isle of Man parliament.

On the edge of Castletown's inner harbour is the Manx Nautical Museum, which includes a sailmaker's workshop and model ships ranging from mid 18th-century sailing craft to modern diesel vessels. Among the exhibits is *Peggy*, last in a line of clippers made in the Isle of Man in the 17th and 18th centuries.

CALF OF MAN ➡ Calf of Man can be reached in summer by regular boat trips from Port Erin and Port St Mary.
CASTLETOWN ➡ 10 miles SW of Douglas.

To the south of Castletown is the Scarlett Visitor Centre, which has displays of the island's plants and animals, and a nature trail that follows part of the coastline.

DHOON GLEN One of the most spectacular glens on the Isle of Man,
Dhoon Glen is formed by a fast-running stream that cuts its way down through the cliffs to the sea at Dhoon Bay. The path to the shore crosses the glen by a series of rustic bridges, passing two steep waterfalls, each of which drops 18m (59ft) or more.

LAXEY One of the Isle of Man's best-known sights is the huge Laxey Wheel, a mighty water wheel,
also known as the Lady Isabella. It was constructed in 1854 to pump water out of the lead-mine workings under Snaefell, the island's highest mountain, and was named after the wife of the then lieutenant governor of the island. It has a diameter of 22m (72½ft) and a circumference of 66m (217ft), and it still pumps water – when running at top speed a complete revolution takes 30 seconds. Visitors can follow trails past former mine workings.

On the opposite side of the valley from the wheel, the Snaefell Mountain Railway runs in a long spiral up to the 621m (2,037ft) summit of Snaefell. The journey, which takes about half an hour, ends at a spectacular viewpoint.

DHOON GLEN ➡ 10 miles NE of Douglas.
LAXEY ➡ 8 miles NE of Douglas.

PEEL An old fishing harbour, with narrow, winding streets, is dominated by the massive fortress of Peel Castle on St Patrick's Isle. The 'isle' is in fact linked to the mainland, forming a protective arm at the western end of the harbour. The castle's main walls are 14th-century, and within are a huge round tower and a ruined 13th-century cathedral.

On the eastern side of the harbour a promenade overlooks a sandy beach. There is good fishing for mackerel at the entrance to the harbour, and for mullet, skate, pollack, conger eel and flatfish from the breakwater beyond the castle. Manx kippers, cured over fires of oak woodchips, are produced in the town.

Tynwald Hill, 3 miles southeast of Peel at St John's, was the traditional meeting place of Tynwald, the island's parliament, which has its origins in Viking times. Tynwald still meets there on July 5 each year, to hear details of the year's new Acts, which are read in both Manx and English by the island's two deemsters, or high court judges.

RAMSEY The mild climate of Ramsey, and its sheltered position in the centre of the long sweep of Ramsey Bay, allows palm trees to grow on the seafront. Pleasure craft pack the harbour, in the estuary of the Sulby, and there are sandy beaches on either side of the river mouth.

Ramsey is the northern terminus of the Manx Electric Railway, whose trams run south to Douglas via Laxey.

PEEL ➡ 12 miles NW of Douglas.
RAMSEY ➡ 15 miles N of Douglas.

Lancashire

AINSDALE SAND DUNES High rolling dune ridges, valleys and hollows characterise the national nature reserve that lies at the centre of one of Britain's largest dune systems, stretching from Southport to Crosby.

A marked trail traces a circular route through the sands, where display boards describe the local wildlife and landscape. Natterjack toads live in the low hollows, known as slacks, in the dunes; on spring and summer nights, the mating calls of the male toads create such a chorus that they have been nicknamed the 'Southport nightingales'. You can hear them by joining a guided Natterjack Night Walk organised by the reserve. Wading birds flock to the beach and dune area, and the reserve supports many sand-loving plants, such as dune helleborine and yellow bartsia, as well as butterflies.

The 21-mile Sefton Coastal Footpath runs the length of the dunes, from Crossens in the north to Crosby Marine Park in the south. Industrial and urban development has destroyed part of the dunes, which once stretched all the way from the mouth of the Ribble to Liverpool. But repair work started in the late 1970s, and marram grass has been planted to stabilise them. Flood banks also protect the land behind the dunes from tidal surges. Just inland, large pine plantations from the early 1900s provide habitats for a variety of wildlife, including red squirrels.

AINSDALE SAND DUNES ➡ W of A565 between Southport and Formby.

BLACKPOOL More than 10 million visits are made to Blackpool each year, the visitors drawn by attractions including the 158m (518ft) Tower and huge Pleasure Beach, with some 150 rides. Every inch of the seafront between the North and South piers is packed with hotels, bars, pubs and entertainments. There are 3,500 hotels, guest houses and self-catering units in the resort.

From early September to early November the illuminations dispel the autumn darkness with more than 500,000 lamps. The best way to see them is from one of the trams that trundle along the seafront to Cleveleys and on to Fleetwood.

COCKERSAND ABBEY Cows graze among the scattered ruins of Cockersand Abbey, once one of the great religious houses in northwest England. The squat tower of the 13th-century chapter house, and a few stunted walls, are all that remain of the abbey, built in the early 12th century on a remote tip of land at the mouth of the River Lune. At low tide, you can also see the remnants of a fish trap built by the monks.

A few hundred yards from the shore is a small lighthouse topped by a black cone. The bulk of Heysham nuclear power station looms on the far shore, and beyond are the Lakeland hills. A narrow lane leads to the shore, from where a pleasant 10-minute stroll brings you to the abbey.

BLACKPOOL ➨ 15 miles W of Preston. M6 (Junction 32), then M55.
COCKERSAND ABBEY ➨ 6 miles S of Lancaster on minor roads off A588.

FORMBY HILLS The high grassy dunes were planted with Scots pine in the late 19th century and are now a nature reserve and home to a thriving colony of red squirrels and the rare natterjack toad. As the tide goes out over the flats, it sometimes reveals fossilised Neolithic footprints, which date back 5,000 or more years. More than 160 human trails have been recorded here.

HEYSHAM High on a headland, looking out across Morecambe Bay's sands, stand a cluster of solitary graves, including one of a child, cut out of the rock. The graves stand beside the ruins of tiny St Patrick's Chapel, whose thick walls were built in the 8th and 9th centuries. Just below the chapel is the Church of St Peter, dating from the 10th century.

RIBBLE MARSHES NATIONAL NATURE RESERVE
Stretching along the south bank of the Ribble estuary are the salt marsh, mudflats and sandbanks of the reserve. Thousands of ducks, geese, gulls and terns depend on the varied habitat for feeding and breeding, and each spring and autumn up to 80,000 waders, including knots, dunlins and oystercatchers, arrive at Ribble Marshes on their way to and from the Arctic. To the north, a footpath leads along Banks Marsh embankment. Spring tides can cause flooding, making the salt marsh dangerous.

FORMBY HILLS ➡ 1 mile W of Formby.
HEYSHAM ➡ 4 miles W of Lancaster on A683.
RIBBLE MARSHES NATIONAL NATURE RESERVE ➡ 3 miles N of Southport.

NORTHEAST

ENGLAND

Northumberland & Tyneside

BAMBURGH An outcrop of rock rises 46m (150ft) above the sandy bay of Bamburgh and continues into the pink stone walls and battlements of majestic Bamburgh Castle, which towers above the village and rolling dunes. Bamburgh became the Northumbrian capital under King Oswald, who ruled in the 7th century, though the castle was later pillaged by the Danes. A deep well, possibly dating from the 8th century, is Bamburgh Castle's oldest feature, and the 12th-century keep retains its original walls, as thick as 3.4m (11ft) in places.

In the churchyard of the fine Early English Church of St Aidan is a memorial to Bamburgh's own heroine, Grace Darling, who is also commemorated by a small museum run by the Royal National Lifeboat Institution. The museum's centrepiece is the fishing coble in which she and her father rescued the crew of the paddle-steamer *Forfarshire* in 1838.

CRASTER Overlooking Craster's little harbour are the smoking sheds where the village's famous kippers are produced. The harbour, which empties of water at low

BAMBURGH ▶ 3 miles N of Seahouses on B1340.
CRASTER ▶ 6 miles NE of Alnwick off A1/B1340.

tide, is now used by leisure boats and a few cobles that fish for lobsters and crabs. Behind the car park is the Arnold Memorial Nature Reserve, where you can sometimes see bluethroats and other rare birds in the lush woodlands.

DRURIDGE BAY A 6-mile crescent of sandy beach, backed by grass-covered dunes, is the setting for an environmental effort aimed at protecting and enhancing wildlife habitats.Until 1989, Ladyburn Lake, in Druridge Bay Country Park, was an opencast mine; it is now a venue for watersports. The park, which has a large visitor centre, embraces 3½ miles of beach and dunes, with rocks and rock pools at its northern end.

DUNSTANBURGH CASTLE The commanding ruins of the castle are perched on a ledge of basalt rock. The only way to reach Dunstanburgh Castle (NT/EH) is by foot – cars should be parked at Craster to the south. Northumberland's most ethereal and enigmatic castle, it was begun in 1313 by Thomas, Earl of Lancaster. The original great gatehouse, with twin towers and walls, was converted into a keep in 1380 by John of Gaunt, once the most powerful man in England. From the top of one of the towers, there are panoramic views down the steep incline of the castle rock to the rolling fields beyond.

DRURIDGE BAY ➡ 5 miles N of Ashington off A1068.
DUNSTANBURGH CASTLE ➡ Paths from Craster or Embleton, off B1339.

FARNE ISLANDS A scattering of rocky offshore outcrops, the Farne Islands (NT) form a nature reserve

that attracts nesting seabirds, including puffins, kittiwakes and terns. They are also one of the grey seal's principal breeding grounds. The largest of 28 islands is Inner Farne, where in AD 676 St Cuthbert built himself a cell of stone and turf and lived alone for eight years. A 14th-century chapel dedicated to him stands near Prior Castell's Tower, built in 1500. Boats tour the islands from Seahouses harbour.

HOLY ISLAND The fretted and worn red sandstone ruins of Lindesfarne Priory (EH) stand on a wide peninsula of sand,

which is cut off from the mainland for 11 out of 24 hours at high tide. Christianity came to the island in AD 634, when the monk Aidan crossed the sands to found a monastery, subsequently destroyed by the Danes. One relic survived the attack, the Lindisfarne Gospels, a masterpiece of English Celtic art, and now one of the treasures of the British Library. Lindisfarne Priory was begun in 1093, and the priory museum portrays the life of the isolated Holy Island monks.

Outside the priory walls lie the tight-knit houses of Lindisfarne village. Beyond the harbour, Lindisfarne Castle (NT) is dramatically sited on a cone of rock. Built in 1550, it was restored from ruins in 1902 by the architect Edwin Lutyens. On the north side of the island, dunes back onto sandy beaches.

FARNE ISLANDS ➡ Off Seahouses, B1340, 14 miles NE of Alnwick.
HOLY ISLAND ➡ 7 miles S of Berwick-upon-Tweed off A1. Causeway impassable at high tide.

JARROW

JARROW **The ruins of a Saxon monastery where the Venerable Bede lived and worked** can be traced in the ruins of a later Norman foundation in this small riverside town. Above the chancel arch of St Paul's Church is the original Saxon dedication stone of AD 685, and one of the windows in the chancel contains stained glass from the same period, made in the monastic workshops. Nearby, Bede's World tells the story of Northumbria in the early Middle Ages; the museum includes a reconstruction of an Anglo-Saxon farm.

The town has earned a place in history on two other accounts: the hunger marchers set out from Jarrow in 1936 and the novelist Catherine Cookson was born there in 1906.

LINDISFARNE NATIONAL NATURE RESERVE

LINDISFARNE NATIONAL NATURE RESERVE **A vast area of dunes, salt marsh and mudflats,** the reserve stretches from Goswick Sands in the north to Budle Bay in the south. It is internationally known for the large flocks of wildfowl and waders, and in winter the sheltered waters round Holy Island teem with ducks, geese – including pale-bellied Brent geese from Svalbard – and whooper swans. Bar-tailed godwits, redshanks and dunlin are among the more common waders that winter on the flats. You can also see grey and common seals here sometimes. Insects appreciate the duneland habitat, including grayling butterflies and brown-lipped snails. A 3-mile nature trail leads through the reserve.

JARROW ▐▶ 5 miles E of Newcastle upon Tyne.
LINDISFARNE NATIONAL NATURE RESERVE ▐▶ 10 miles S of Berwick-upon-Tweed off A1.

ROSS BACK SANDS The 3-mile stretch of deserted sands give wonderful views of the fairytale outlines of Lindisfarne Castle and Bamburgh Castle in the foreground. To protect the environment, visitors are not widely encouraged onto this splendid sandy beach, which makes up part of the Lindisfarne National Nature Reserve. But it can be reached after a mile-long walk across the rolling dunes of Ross Links.

TYNEMOUTH The atmospheric ruins of Tynemouth Priory and Castle (EH) stand high on a grassy headland north of the River Tyne. The fortified priory was built in 1090 on the site of a 7th-century monastery destroyed by raiding Dane. With battlemented walls and a powerful gatehouse, it was in military use until after the Second World War, and you can still see the gun battery and magazine. Parts of the sturdy walls enveloping the headland and the priory survive, as does the soaring east end of the priory church and a 15th-century chapel built for the earls of Northumberland.

Below the priory, a huge statue of Newcastle-born Admiral Collingwood, Nelson's second-in-command at Trafalgar, gazes out over the Tyne. A fine wide street of mainly 18th-century houses leads up to the priory gates. On the promenade, which extends northwards along the wide beach of Long Sands, is the Blue Reef Aquarium with its captive-bred colony of harbour seals and walk-through tropical coral-reef tank.

ROSS BACK SANDS ➡ Footpath from Ross, 3 miles NE of Belford, off A1.
TYNEMOUTH ➡ 8 miles E of Newcastle upon Tyne.

There are fine views along the coast

WARKWORTH Enclosed by a horseshoe loop of the meandering Coquet, Warkworth's main street leads steeply up from the river to its splendid 15th-century castle (EH), set high on a grassy mound; Harry Hotspur was born there in 1364. A short walk upstream leads to a landing stage on the south bank of the Coquet, from where English Heritage's only ferryman rows visitors to the Hermitage, a 14th-century chapel cut out of a cliff.

The Northumberland Coast Path heads north from Warkworth along the sands to Alnmouth Bay.

WHITLEY BAY Sheltered from the open sea by rocks, the beach of Whitley Sands is linked to St Mary's Island by a causeway, which can be crossed on foot at low tide. There are fine views along the coast from the top of the 37m (120ft) tall lighthouse, built in 1898. Exhibitions in the visitor centre focus on the history of the lighthouse and the surrounding nature reserve with its rock pools.

Connected with Newcastle by the Tyne and Wear Metro railway, Whitley Bay is the city's main seaside lung. Hotels and guest houses line the seafront, and gardens decorate the slopes between the road and the beach.

The former small fishing village of Cullercoats, just to the south, has been absorbed by Whitley Bay. A cluster of old houses survives round the stone walls of the tiny harbour.

WARKWORTH ▶▶ 6 miles SE of Alnwick on A1068.
WHITLEY BAY ▶▶ 8 miles NE of Newcastle upon Tyne.

Yorkshire

BEMPTON CLIFFS In summer the perpendicular cliffs are home to more than 200,000 birds, including kittiwakes, gannets, razorbills and puffins. A lane from the modern village of Bempton leads through cornfields to the cliffs, where an RSPB visitor centre together with viewpoint information boards give information on the birds that you can see there. As well as seabirds, corn buntings and meadow pipits breed in the grassland and fields on the clifftop.

Cruises offering the best views of the cliffs leave from North Landing and Bridlington during summer.

FLAMBOROUGH HEAD The arrow-shaped headland gets its name from the Saxon 'flean', meaning dart. In Flamborough village, a street of fishermen's cottages and a market-place memorial are reminders of a fishing tradition that dates back to the 9th century. The road from the village passes the Old Tower, a lighthouse built in 1674, and continues to a lighthouse built in 1806, which is open to visitors in summer.

Steep steps descend the slopes to the chalk beach of Selwicks (pronounced 'Silex') Bay, where the sea has carved inlets and sea stacks out of the face of the cliff. A mile's walk over the headland leads to North Landing.

BEMPTON CLIFFS ➡ 5 miles N of Bridlington off B1229.
FLAMBOROUGH HEAD ➡ 5 miles NE of Bridlington on B1259.

HUMBER BRIDGE The monumental Humber Bridge was the longest single-span bridge in the world when it was completed in 1981. Built over the course of eight years, it measures 1,410m (4,626ft) and its two towers stand 155m (510ft) above their supporting platforms. It took 44,120 miles of wire to make the cables, and 480,000 tonnes of concrete to build its two towers and roadway.

Today, the two-lane dual carriageway over the bridge is used by some six million vehicles a year. There is a toll for motor vehicles, but the crossing is free for walkers and cyclists, and the bridge gives you magnificent views up and down the Humber estuary.

ROBIN HOOD'S BAY Stone cottages with red pantiled roofs hug the steep slopes overlooking the bay with which the village shares its name. The narrow, cobbled streets and stepped paths twisting down to the sea here were thick with smuggling activity in the 18th century. Today, visitors must park at the top of the village and walk down.

In the 19th century, Bay Town as it is also known, outranked Whitby as a fishing centre. The museum on Fisherhead recalls local seafaring life and contains displays of the area's fossils and wildlife. Bay Town is at the eastern end of the 190-mile Coast to Coast Walk from St Bees in Cumbria. Bearing southeast, the Cleveland Way leads along exhilarating clifftops.

HUMBER BRIDGE ➡ 6 miles W of Kingston upon Hull.
ROBIN HOOD'S BAY ➡ 5 miles S of Whitby off A171 Scarborough road.

SALTWICK BAY Steep steps lead down the cliffside, which has been hollowed out by alum workings. Good fossils may sometimes be found in the rocks on either side of the bay. The Cleveland Way leads east from Whitby along the clifftop to a small stretch of sand between the rocky promontories of Saltwick Nab and Black Nab.

SPURN HEAD The sand and shingle Spurn peninsula, 3 miles long but in places just 9m (30ft) wide, curves in a great hook into the mouth of the Humber. The peninsula, bordered by a sandy beach on the seaward side and by mudflats on the Humber side, is formed from material washed out from eroding shores to the north. Re-formed over the centuries, it is held in its present precarious position and shape by sea defences.

Since 1960, the Spurn peninsula has been a nature reserve, and it is now designated as Heritage Coast. The spit is a major site from which to observe bird migration, especially in autumn when visiting birds include Brent geese and arctic terns. You may also see seals and porpoises. There is a charge for drivers using the road to Spurn Head; to prevent disturbance to wildlife, dogs are not allowed on the reserve, even in cars. The remains of military defences can also be seen near the car park.

The country's only full-time lifeboat crew live at Spurn Head, and a jetty is the departure point for the pilots who accompany ships navigating the narrow Humber shipping lanes.

SALTWICK BAY ➡ 1 mile E of Whitby.
SPURN HEAD ➡ 2 miles SE of Easington at end of B1445, off A1033 Hull-Withernsea road.

STAITHES James Cook was a haberdasher's apprentice in Staithes in the mid 1740s, when 50 fishing cobles sailed out daily from the village. In the 19th century, Staithes could fill three trains a week with cod, haddock and mackerel. Only a few cobles still fish regularly. Interest in Captain Cook is tapped by a heritage centre, sited in a refurbished former chapel built for Primitive Methodists in 1880. Near the centre is the start of a circular walk to Port Mulgrave, taking two to three hours.

Staithes is reached via a narrow valley that leads to a small harbour, surrounded by cliffs and protected from the open sea by a breakwater and a protective wall of boulders. From the top of the hill near the entrance to the village, streets of closely packed houses wind steeply down to the harbour. Separating them are alleys with names such as Slippery Hill and Gun Gutter.

WHITBY The stark brooding ruins of 13th-century Whitby Abbey (EH) have a spectacular setting on a clifftop above the town. The abbey was built on the site of an earlier monastery dedicated to St Hilda, which housed monks and nuns and produced nine saints, five bishops and the Saxon poet Caedmon.

The large Church of St Mary, beside the abbey, has a Norman tower but was substantially altered in Georgian times. The clifftop graveyard is set with straggling rows of headstones, pock-marked with salt erosion, and can be reached from the harbour below by a steep flight of 199 steps.

STAITHES ➡ 10 miles NW of Whitby off A174.
WHITBY ➡ 20 miles N of Scarborough on A171.

Steps, graveyard and abbey ruins all feature in Bram Stoker's novel *Dracula*, and melodramatic tastes are catered for at the Dracula Experience on Marine Parade.

The harbour town's setting can be viewed in a sweeping panorama from the bridge that spans the estuary of the Esk. The river divides the eastern side of the town from the Victorian West Cliff development. Surveying the lively harbour from the western side is the statue of Captain Cook, whose great ships of exploration were all built at Whitby. The Captain Cook Memorial Museum, set in a house where Cook once lodged, has rooms containing furniture of the period, model ships, and drawings from artists who travelled on the explorer's voyages.

Near the statue of Captain Cook is an arch made from the jawbone of a whale, erected to commemorate what was one of Whitby's major businesses in the 18th and 19th centuries. Local captain William Scoresby, inventor of the crow's-nest ship's lookout, accounted for an extraordinary 533 whales in his career. Whitby remains a working fishing port, and herrings are still smoked over oak to produce kippers.

Whitby Museum in Pannett Park has one of Britain's finest fossil collections as well as jewellery carved from jet found on the local shore. You can also visit the Museum of Victorian Whitby and the Lifeboat Museum in Pier Road.

Holiday activities include sailing, sea and river fishing, and seaside amusements on the fine Whitby Sands. Two miles inland, at Ruswarp, you can hire rowing boats to explore the Esk.

WALES

North & Mid Wales

BARDSEY ISLAND NATIONAL NATURE RESERVE

The remote mass of rock, dominated by a 167m (548ft) hill, is 2 miles from the mainland across a sound seething with strong currents. In Welsh, Bardsey is called Ynys Enlli, or Isle of the Eddies. It became a refuge for early Christians after the Romans left Britain and later was an important pilgrimage site. So many pilgrims were buried there that it also became known as the Isle of Twenty Thousand Saints.

Bardsey Island is now a national nature reserve, and farmhouses have been converted into holiday accommodation. Day visits can be made from Aberdaron by booking a place on the boat a few days ahead.

BARMOUTH Clinging to the hillside above the harbour, the old town is a maze of cottages and slate-stepped alleyways, while the seafront of this popular holiday resort has sandy beaches, donkey rides and bright arcades. On the quayside is Ty Gwyn, a small museum housed in a 15th-century building, which contains artefacts from a local Tudor shipwreck. Nearby, Ty Crwn is a circular lock-up house built in 1834.

A trail leads from the old town to the viewpoint of Dinas Olau, which in 1895 was the first piece of land to

BARDSEY ISLAND NATIONAL NATURE RESERVE ➡➡ Off W tip of Lleyn Peninsula.
BARMOUTH ➡➡ 10 miles W of Dolgellau on A496.

be acquired by the National Trust. A 4-mile track dubbed the Panorama Walk skirts the hills overlooking the Mawddach estuary and leads to the hamlet of Cutiau.

The railway bridge across the estuary has a pedestrian walkway, and a ferry service connects with the Fairbourne & Barmouth Steam Railway.

BEAUMARIS

Built by Edward I, Beaumaris Castle (Cadw), is one of Britain's most sophisticated examples of medieval military architecture and dominates the fine little town. The 13th-century castle's moat was originally linked to the sea, and two rings of walls are punctuated by defensive towers. Other buildings of note in the town include the Grammar School of 1603, the Courthouse of 1614 – still in use and open for visits in summer – and the nearby early 19th-century jail.

CARMEL HEAD

Anglesey's remote northwestern corner drops away to the sea in steep cliffs. Offshore are The Skerries with their lighthouse, built in 1841. It replaced a fire in a brazier kept burning by a husband and wife who lived out on the rocks to maintain this lonely duty.

Carmel Head (NT) is reached by a footpath sited by a sharp bend in the road north of Llanfairynghornwy. You may spot choughs and peregrine falcons here on the cliffs.

BEAUMARIS ➡ 4 miles NE of Menai Bridge on A545.
CARMEL HEAD ➡ 15 miles N of Holyhead off A5025.

CONWY Immense, well-preserved walls enclose the town and castle (Cadw) of Conwy, making it Britain's finest medieval fortified town. The walls run for nearly a mile, broken up by 21 jutting bastions every 46m (50yd).

Between 1283 and 1289, some 1,500 craftsmen constructed massive Conwy Castle for Edward I, with a barbican at either end and eight tall towers. From the ramparts of the castle there are good views down to the crowded streets below and out over the Conwy estuary.

A wealth of old buildings located within the walls includes the 14th-century timber-framed Aberconwy House (NT) and 16th-century Plas Mawr (Cadw), which is distinctive for its ornate plasterwork. On the quayside, overlooking a collection of fishing boats, is what is said to be the smallest house in Britain, with a frontage just 2.5m (8ft 2in) in height and 1.8m (6ft) across. Pleasure cruises and sea-fishing trips leave from the quay.

Four crossings link the two banks of the river. Thomas Telford's 1820s suspension bridge is now used by pedestrians only. The other three are a tubular rail bridge designed by Robert Stephenson in the 1840s, a road bridge and a road tunnel carrying the Conwy bypass.

North of the town is a marina surrounded by a residential development, and the wide sands of Morfa Beach. On the north bank of the Conwy estuary at Llandudno Junction is an RSPB reserve, accessed from the A55. Godwits and shelducks are among the 200 species spotted at the reserve.

CONWY ➟ 4 miles S of Llandudno on A55.

Some 1,500 craftsmen constructed massive Conwy Castle

CRICCIETH The ruins of Criccieth Castle (Cadw) stand high on a towering headland, overlooking the Victorian terraces of the little town of Criccieth on one side and the open sea on the other. Constructed by the Welsh prince Llywelyn ap Gruffydd in the middle of the 13th century, the fortress passed into English hands when Edward I captured it in 1283. It was retaken by Owain Glyndwr during his rebellion in 1404. Some of the cracks and splits in the stonework probably date from the final siege, when the castle was sacked and burnt by the Welsh.

DYFFRYN ARDUDWY Seven miles of sandy beach, backed by grass-covered dunes, stretch from Shell Island to Barmouth passing this village. To the northwest is the unspoilt Morfa Dyffryn Nature Reserve. On the southern outskirts of the village are the remains of a prehistoric burial chamber, managed by Cadw, and many other sites lie in the nearby hills. Pony-trekking is available.

GREAT ORMES HEAD The headland rises as a great rocky pile to a 207m (679ft) summit at the northeastern end of Conwy Bay. If you want to reach the top without walking, you have three options: to go by car along the Marine Drive toll road; to take the cable car; or to use Britain's last

CRICCIETH ➡ 5 miles W of Porthmadog on A497.
DYFFRYN ARDUDWY ➡ 5 miles N of Barmouth on A496.
GREAT ORMES HEAD ➡ 1 mile NW of Llandudno off minor road, or tramway to Orme summit.

cable-hauled street tramway, opened in 1902. Copper was mined at Great Ormes Head in the 18th and 19th centuries, but recent excavations have uncovered mines that were first worked around 1800 BC, during the Bronze Age. The tramway stops at the mines, where you can explore the old workings.

At the summit there is a country park with a visitor centre offering tremendous views over Snowdonia to the south and, on clear days, to the mountains of Cumbria some 60 miles north. On the sheltered eastern slopes are the public gardens of Haulfre, with good views of the sands of both Llandudno and West Shore, and on the exposed northern face is the little 7th-century church and well of St Tudno, after whom Llandudno was named.

HARLECH One of Edward I's string of fortresses, Harlech Castle (Cadw) stands dramatically on a 61m (200ft) rocky bluff. In 1404, it was captured by Owain Glyndwr, who based his court here until it was retaken by the English five years later. During the Wars of the Roses, it was held by the Lancastrians and withstood a seven-year siege by the Yorkists before falling in 1468. The song 'Men of Harlech' is said to have been inspired by the Lancastrians' resistance.

The small town of Harlech is built along a ridge behind the castle bluff, and to the west paths cross high dunes to a large sandy beach. Nearby is Royal St David's golf course.

HARLECH ➡ 16 miles S of Porthmadog on A496.

HOLYHEAD MOUNTAIN At 219m (720ft), this is the highest hill in Anglesey.

On the summit are the remains of the Iron Age fort of Caer y Twr (Cadw), which houses the ruins of a 4th-century Roman watchtower or beacon. On the lower slopes to the west is the settlement of Cytiau'r Gwyddelod (Cadw), inhabited during the 3rd and 4th centuries. The low stone walls of 20 huts survive, some showing where the inhabitants placed their fires, seats and beds.

LLANDDWYN BAY The 4-mile stretch of sand in the bay gives spectacular views across the Menai Strait

to the mountains of Snowdonia. The sands are bordered by a vast area of dunes to the east and Newborough Forest to the west, which offers a number of forest walks.

Llanddwyn Island, technically a peninsula rather than an island, forms part of the Newborough Warren National Nature Reserve. The island is named after St Dwynwen, patron saint of Welsh lovers, who founded a convent there in the 5th century. Crosses commemorate the saint and her followers, and ruins survive of a Tudor church built on the site of her chapel. At the tip of the island is a disused 19th-century lighthouse, standing beside the cottages that once belonged to pilots who guided vessels over the sandbars at the entrance to the Menai Strait. One of the houses has been restored to show how it would have looked around 1900; it is open for visitors in summer.

HOLYHEAD MOUNTAIN ➡ 2 miles W of Holyhead.
LLANDDWYN BAY ➡ Access via toll road from Newborough on A4080.

NEWBOROUGH WARREN Thyme and marsh orchids thrive in the unforested dunes and wet hollows of the warren, which is now a national nature reserve. Waders and wildfowl overwinter on the mudflats and salt marshes, and Ynys yr Adar is a breeding site for cormorants. The small freshwater lake of Llyn Rhos Ddu on the reserve attracts ducks, grebes, coots and moorhens.

Violent storms in the Middle Ages covered with sand what was once a huge area of farmland in southern Anglesey. In Tudor times the dunes were stabilised by planting marram grass; more recently, Newborough Warren, as the area became known, was home to a huge colony of rabbits, until the animals were almost wiped out by myxomatosis in 1954.

PENMON Carved Celtic crosses and a 1,000-year-old font are some of the treasures to be seen in the ruins of Penmon Priory. According to tradition, St Seiriol, a son of the ruler of the north Welsh kingdom of Rhos, founded a priory here in the 6th century. After the original building was destroyed by Viking raiders, the priory was rebuilt in the 12th century and much of the Norman architecture survives. Nearby are the spring of St Seiriol's Well, said to have been used by the hermit saint, and a 17th-century dovecote.

A toll road leads past some disused quarries to Trwyn Du (Black Point) and spectacular views across Conwy Bay.

NEWBOROUGH WARREN ➡ 2 miles SW of Newborough off A4080 Llanfair PG-Rhosneigr road.
PENMON ➡ 4 miles N of Beaumaris off B5109.

PENRHYN CASTLE An extravagant example of the early 19th-century taste for neo-Norman architecture, the castle (NT) was designed in 1820 by Thomas Hopper for the Pennant family. Inside are elaborate stone carvings and an exhibition of paintings by old masters, such as Rembrandt and Canaletto. The stables house a doll museum and a collection of industrial locomotives, and the lush grounds include a ruined medieval chapel and pet cemetery.

You can see kingfishers, peregrine falcons and firecrests at the Spinnies Nature Reserve, to the east of the castle.

PLAS NEWYDD A mixture of classical and Gothic styles, Plas Newydd (NT) stands in an imposing position on the banks of the Menai Strait. The mansion was built in the 1790s by James Wyatt and Joseph Potter for the Paget family, later the Marquesses of Anglesey. Among the relics on display is the artificial leg of the first Marquess of Anglesey, Wellington's second-in-command at Waterloo. In the dining room is an immense mural, 18m (58ft) wide, painted by Rex Whistler in the 1930s. The house is set in beautiful gardens with an Italianate terrace and Australasian arboretum, and views across the Strait to Snowdonia. There are woodland walks and a marine walk along the Menai Strait.

PENRHYN CASTLE ➡ 1 mile E of Bangor off A5.
PLAS NEWYDD ➡ 2 miles SW of Llanfair PG on A4080 Newborough road.

PORTMEIRION Buildings in extravagant Italianate style rub shoulders with architectural oddments brought from all over Britain in this fantasy folly on the grandest scale. Inspired by a visit to the Italian resort of Portofino in the 1920s, the architect Sir Clough Williams-Ellis returned home determined to create a 'dream village'. Built in stages between 1925 and 1972, Portmeirion consists of 50 buildings, a central plaza and tiny harbour. It includes a tall bell-tower, built by Williams-Ellis, and an 18th-century colonnade salvaged from Bristol. In the 1960s, the television series *The Prisoner* was filmed here.

The village overlooks the Dwyryd estuary, and footpaths lead through gardens of subtropical plants and trees to a sandy beach. Strong currents and tides make swimming dangerous.

SOUTH STACK Holy Island's northwestern tip consists of a huge rock, crowned by a lighthouse, with 61m (200ft) cliffs. You reach the island by descending some 400 stone steps, then crossing over an aluminium bridge. The cliffs at South Stack, part of an RSPB nature reserve, are noted for their vast numbers of seabirds, including a colony of puffins. Standing on the rockface to the south of the lighthouse, crenellated Twr Elin, or Ellin's Tower, was built in the 18th century as a summerhouse by the Stanleys of Alderley. It is now the reserve's visitor centre. Clifftop walks lead northeast around Gogarth Bay to the promontory of North Stack.

PORTMEIRION ➡ 3 miles E of Porthmadog off A487.
SOUTH STACK ➡ 3 miles W of Holyhead on minor roads.

WALES

South Wales

ABEREIDDY **In a former slate quarry, a deep sheer-sided pool called the Blue Lagoon** now provides a sheltered and romantic anchorage for small boats. It is reached by a short path from Abereiddy past ruined cottages.

Slate-grey sands create an unusual beach on the fine west-facing bay of Abereiddy. To the north are isolated sandy beaches beneath the cliffs at Traethllyfn.

CALDEY ISLAND **A cross with an inscription in the Celtic ogham alphabet is a reminder** that the island was first inhabited by monks in the 6th century. The Benedictines arrived in the 12th century and remained on the island until the dissolution of the monasteries by Henry VIII. Surviving buildings that date from this time include the gatehouse and the Prior's Lodging. Monastic life resumed in 1906, and the rebuilt monastery is now home to Cistercian monks.

You can visit wooded Caldey Island by boat from Tenby during summer. Once there, you can see the churches, buy the perfume and chocolate made by the monks, or simply enjoy the calm. Only male visitors may enter the monastery itself.

There are splendid views of colonies of seals and seabirds from the top of the hill that crowns the island.

ABEREIDDY ➡➡ 5 miles NE of St David's off A487.
CALDEY ISLAND ➡➡ Crossings from Tenby, 9 miles E of Pembroke on A4139.

DINAS HEAD

DINAS HEAD Jutting out between Fishguard Bay and Newport Bay, the stubby peninsula of Dinas Head provides a 3-mile circular walk along the cliffs and through Cwm Dewi, the sheltered valley that divides it from the mainland. Cwm-yr-Eglwys, the village at the eastern end of Cwm Dewi, has a sandy beach and is a good starting point for walks. The village's ruined St Brynach's Church was a victim of a great storm of 1859, which in a single night wrecked more than 100 ships off the Welsh coast.

Pwllgwaelod, situated to the west of Cwm Dewi, is a beach of sand and rocks.

ELEGUG STACKS

ELEGUG STACKS Two great limestone pillars rear up out of the waves beside high cliffs. In the summer breeding season, guillemots arrive in great flocks, perching on the ledges and jostling for space with an array of auks, razorbills, fulmars and kittiwakes.

Just to the west, a natural rock arch, known as the Green Bridge of Wales, thrusts out from the cliffs, while the headland immediately to the east shows traces of the defensive ditches and ramparts of an Iron Age fort. When Castlemartin Range is not in use, visitors can enjoy an exhilarating walk along the dramatic cliff path east from Elegug Stacks to St Govan's Head.

DINAS HEAD ➡ 6 miles NE of Fishguard off A487.
ELEGUG STACKS ➡ 8 miles S of Pembroke off B4319.

Dramatic cliffs and rock formations rise
from golden sands

MARLOES SANDS You can reach one of Britain's finest beaches, where dramatic cliffs and rock formations rise from golden sands, by a 10-minute walk from the car park west of Marloes village. Marloes Mere, to the west of the beach, was once famous for its leeches, which were gathered for sale to London doctors in the 18th century.

MERTHYR MAWR This delightful village of thatched stone-built cottages lies scattered along tree-shaded lanes by the banks of the River Ogmore. One narrow lane leads to Candleston Castle, a 15th-century fortified manor house, now largely ruined. Some interesting details of the castle survive, such as the carved fireplace of the great hall. Separating the hamlet from the sea are the immense sand dunes known as the Merthyr-mawr Warren. Paths through the desert-like dunes lead to the sandy beach of Traeth yr Afon, but currents near the mouth of the Ogmore make swimming dangerous.

Just south of Merthyr Mawr are the lonely ruins of another fortress – Ogmore Castle, reached by stepping stones across the river. The castle was built by the Norman invader William de Londres in the 12th century. The keep, built of massive boulders, is slightly later.

In Ewenny, a riverside village about a mile to the east, are the remains of a fortified priory founded in the 12th century, and the workshops of the Ewenny Pottery, one of Wales's oldest.

MARLOES SANDS ➡ 14 miles SW of Haverfordwest off B4327.
METHYR MAWR ➡ 3 miles SW of Bridgend on minor roads.

PENDINE SANDS Firm, flat sands stretch for 6 miles from the holiday village of Pendine to the Taf estuary. At low tide, the sea can be a mile or more away from the foreshore, while the long expanse of shallow water at high tide makes it very popular with young families. The beach was used in the 1920s in several attempts to break the land-speed record, and was the site of Parry Thomas's fatal crash in 1927.

East of Pendine is a Ministry of Defence firing range, but the sands are usually open to the public most weekends and from 5pm on weekdays.

RAMSEY ISLAND RSPB RESERVE Boats to this superb bird sanctuary of cliffs and mountain heath depart in summer from St Justinian. Guillemots, razorbills and kittiwakes nest on 122m (400ft) precipices above isolated coves where grey seals breed, while fields grazed by sheep and deer provide a perfect habitat for birds such as lapwings.

RHOSSILI BAY & WORMS HEAD A magnificent crescent of flat sand, with a creamy edge of curling surf, is set against a background of imposing cliffs at Rhossili Bay. The steep climb from the village down to the shore ensures that the beach is never as crowded as some of the more easily reached beaches on the Gower. It provides good

PENDINE SANDS ➠ 15 miles E of Tenby.
RAMSEY ISLAND RSPB RESERVE ➠ Crossings from St Justinian, signposted from St David's on A487.
RHOSSILI BAY & WORMS HEAD ➠ 18 miles W of Swansea at end of B4247.

surfing conditions, and the surrounding cliffs are popular with paragliders and hang-gliders. Heather and bracken-covered Rhossili Down (NT), rising up behind the cliffs, is an excellent area for walks.

A line of rocks, Worms Head snakes out from the headland to form part of the Gower Coast National Nature Reserve, which stretches east as far as Port-Eynon. Worms Head can be reached with care during the four hours either side of low tide. The best starting point for a walk is the National Trust visitor centre just outside Rhossili village. From there a path leads for 3 miles over the cliffs, with superb views across Rhossili Bay. The two islands at the seaward end of the head are joined by a rock arch called the Devil's Bridge, where in high winds an eerie booming noise can be heard. This is caused by air rushing through the hole.

SEVERN BRIDGES With a main span of 988m (3,240ft), and towers that reach 136m (445ft) in height,

the first Severn Bridge was completed in 1966. Before the bridge was built, the only way to cross the river with a vehicle was by a long road detour or by ferry.

To cope with the increase in traffic, a second bridge was constructed 3 miles downstream to carry the M4. Opened in 1996, the overall length of the structure is 5,128m (16,823ft) with a clear span of 456m (1,496ft).

SEVERN BRIDGES ➡ The northern bridge carries the M48 and the southern the M4.

SKOKHOLM ISLAND Smaller and more remote than Skomer, Skokholm was the site of Britain's first bird observatory in 1933. The observatory and some converted farm buildings now provide accommodation for staff and visitors. Manx shearwaters, puffins, razorbills and guillemots are abundant, and the island is a resting place for many migrant species. There is a large colony of storm petrels, too, which like the shearwaters come ashore only to breed and only at night.

The island is bounded by distinctive, deeply coloured old red sandstone cliffs rising to 49m (160ft) in the southwest and topped by a plateau with rocky outcrops.

SKOMER An estimated 165,000 pairs of Manx shearwaters nest in clifftop burrows on this island, the breeding ground of almost half the world's population of these birds. Puffins, guillemots, razorbills and kittiwakes are also common, while grey seals breed in shoreline caves and dolphins fish the tidal races.

Wild flowers, such as sea pinks and yellow samphires, are spectacular in spring and early summer. Skomer is reached by boat from Martin's Haven.

The waters, seabed and shore around Skomer form a marine nature reserve, whose range of habitats supports a great number of creatures and plants, including corals, sponges, sea firs, sea slugs and dogfish.

SKOKHOLM ISLAND ➡➡ Crossings from Martin's Haven, signposted from B4327 via Marloes.
SKOMER ➡➡ Crossings from Martin's Haven, signposted from B4327 via Marloes.

ST DAVID'S The cathedral has a superb setting in a valley beside the massive and ornate ruins of Bishop's Palace (Cadw), which date mainly from the 14th century. An outstanding feature of the palace ruins is an arcaded parapet built by Bishop Henry de Gower.

The smallest of all cathedral cities, St David's was the birthplace of the patron saint of Wales. St David founded a monastery here during the 6th century, and the city became a place of pilgrimage in the Middle Ages. The present cathedral dates largely from the late 12th century, but incorporates later features such as the carved Renaissance ceiling in the nave. An exhibition outlining the history of the cathedral can be seen in the Gatehouse, which is the only remaining one of four gatehouses built into the city wall in the 14th century.

There is an attractively sited golf course on the road to Whitesands Bay. St Non's Chapel (Cadw), south of the city, is traditionally identified as the birthplace of St David's mother, and has a healing well that still attracts visitors.

ST DAVID'S HEAD Stone outcrops rise above wild but beautiful moorland on this peninsula. An ancient route that once linked Pembrokeshire with Salisbury Plain and Ireland leads down to the shore, and there is a Neolithic cromlech (megalith) on the skyline. An Iron Age fort on the headland stands near a stone rampart known as the Warrior's Dyke.

ST DAVID'S ➡ 14 miles NW of Haverfordwest on A487.
ST DAVID'S HEAD ➡ 3 miles NW of St David's. Path from end of B4583 at Whitesands Bay.

ST DONAT'S CASTLE What appears to be a mock-Norman fantasy castle overlooking a bay is in fact a 14th-century fortress, turned into a more comfortable residence during the Elizabethan era with the addition of an inner courtyard and great hall. The castle was neglected from the 18th century until 1925, when the US newspaper magnate William Randolph Hearst took it over and restored the building. He installed such features as a magnificent dining-room ceiling rescued from a Lincolnshire church.

ST GOVAN'S CHAPEL A flight of steep, well-worn stone steps leads down to a tiny church squeezed into a cleft in the rocks. According to tradition, St Govan was being pursued by pirates when the rocks split open to provide a hiding place, and he stayed here preaching and praying until his death in AD 586. The present chapel, however, dates from the 11th century. Outside is a small well, now dry, whose waters were thought to have healing powers.

Legend is also behind the naming of nearby Bell Rock. The church bell, stolen by pirates, was said to have been saved by angels, who set it in the rock. When St Govan struck the boulder, it sounded as loud as a mighty cathedral bell.

To the west is a great gash in the cliffs known as Huntsman's Leap. A huntsman is said to have jumped his horse over this 55m (180ft) cleft – then, on looking back, to have died of fright.

ST DONAT'S CASTLE ➧ 10 miles S of Bridgend on minor roads.
ST GOVAN'S CHAPEL ➧ Bosherston, signposted from B4319,
3 miles S of Pembroke. St Govan's is near a firing range.

TENBY In the town's narrow streets, Georgian villas with intricate iron balconies jostle with fishermen's cottages. The resort's great appeal for holidaymakers lies in its sandy beaches and sheltered bathing, and in its beautiful little harbour crowded with boats. Much of Tenby's present character comes from its development in the 19th century as a watering place by Sir William Paxton, but its origins are much older. Little remains of the Norman castle; most of it was destroyed in the Civil War. But much does survive of the 13th-century town wall, including the old west gate, now known as Five Arches.

The medieval St Mary's Church is enlivened by carved figures looking down from the nave roof and by ornate chancel vaulting. The town's past prosperity is reflected in the refurbished Tudor Merchant's House (NT) and in displays at the museum and art gallery, which also has a section devoted to the work of the Tenby-born artist Augustus John.

On St Catherine's Island, which you can reach on foot at low tide, is a 19th-century fortress, part of the protective ring that once defended the military dockyards of Milford Haven.

THREECLIFF BAY Flanked by limestone cliffs, the bay is one of the most beautiful on the South Wales Coast. The name comes from the three crags that rear up above the beach, one of which forms a rock arch. Threecliff can be reached only on foot from either Parkmill or Southgate.

TENBY ➡ 13 miles E of Pembroke at junction of A478 and A4139.
THREECLIFF BAY ➡ 9 miles W of Swansea off A4118.

SCOTLAND

SCOTLAND

Central & Northeast Scotland

ARBROATH Raucous calls of seabirds announce the early morning fish landings at this port famous for the Arbroath 'smokie' – haddock cured slowly over a beechwood fire. Until the end of the 19th century, the town was principally a trading harbour. Today, Arbroath is a holiday resort, with attractions such as Kerr's Miniature Railway, which has been operating since 1935. Beyond the Kings Drive promenade, Arbroath Cliffs nature trail, leading towards Auchmithie, takes in seabird nesting grounds, wild-flower havens and spectacular rock formations.

Arbroath Abbey (HS), a well-preserved ruin, was built in 1178 and dedicated by the Scottish King William the Lion to his martyred friend Thomas Becket. The Declaration of Arbroath, signed in 1320, was a re-affirmation of Scotland's independence. The Signal Tower now houses an Arbroath history museum.

ARDUAINE GARDEN Rhododendrons, azaleas, shrubberies, lawns and a wilder woodland garden on the higher slopes make up Arduaine Garden (NTS). It is reached from the Loch Melfort Hotel by a path offering views of offshore islands and the marina at Craobh Haven.

ARBROATH ➥ 16 miles NE of Dundee on A92.
ARDUAINE GARDEN ➥ 20 miles S of Oban on A816.

BULLERS OF BUCHAN Visible from the cliff path is a huge granite cauldron called the Pot (or Buller), into which the tide pours through a natural archway. Walkers should take great care walking along the path. Fishermen used to live in the tiny clifftop hamlet, and their boats were kept at the foot of cliffs, where fulmars and kittiwakes nest.

COLONSAY White, empty beaches, standing stones and seal colonies on offshore islets and skerries are some of the attractions of this island. Almost alone among the Hebrides, it suffered no forced evictions during the Highland Clearances and so is free of the sad quality of many other Scottish islands.

Colonsay and its neighbour Oronsay – linked at low tide by a sandy beach – enjoy almost as much sunshine as Tiree, Scotland's record-holder. In northwest Colonsay, Kiloran Bay has one of the island's finest beaches, protected from the full force of the Atlantic by a long headland. At nearby Kiloran Gardens, palm trees and rhododendrons flourish in the mild climate. Wild goats live at the north of Colonsay and on Oronsay; the long-horned, black-fleeced creatures are said to be descended from goats that swam ashore from ships of the Spanish Armada, wrecked here in 1588.

St Columba is said to have landed on Oronsay on his way from Ireland to Iona in the middle of the 6th century. Substantial ruins of a priory date from the 13th century and include tombstones bearing the carved portraits of warriors and priests.

BULLERS OF BUCHAN ➡ 6 miles S of Peterhead off A90.
COLONSAY ➡ Ferry from Oban.

DUNNOTTAR CASTLE The ruined 14th-century fortress stands on an impregnable rock, separated from the mainland by a deep ravine. The castle was involved in many historical episodes and was virtually demolished after the 1715 Jacobite Rising. It was partly restored in 1925. A tunnel entrance leads up towards the top level where the surviving buildings stand.

FINDHORN Grey and common seals live in the bay, and migrating wildfowl visit the tidal mudflats in this former port, now a centre for watersports and sailing. A heritage centre in a converted ice house explains the natural and human history of the area. East of the village, paths lead from the long sandy crescent of Burghead Bay into Roseisle Forest.

FORT GEORGE Standing at the tip of a promontory jutting into the Moray Firth, Fort George is one of Europe's finest 18th-century artillery fortresses. It was built after the Battle of Culloden as a garrison post for the Hanoverian army of George II and is protected by almost a mile of ramparts. Every approach is covered by at least two cannon-lined walls. The fort is still an army barracks, but you may explore several buildings, including the armoury and garrison chapel, and walk the ramparts for views of the Moray Firth. In the grounds is the Regimental Museum of the Queen's Own Highlanders.

DUNNOTTAR CASTLE ➡ 2 miles S of Stonehaven off A92.
FINDHORN ➡ 5 miles N of Forres on B9011.
FORT GEORGE ➡ 11 miles NE of Inverness off A96.

FORVIE NATIONAL NATURE RESERVE Some of the largest dune systems in Britain stretch from Collieston to

the mouth of the River Ythan. A visitor centre in the reserve describes this fascinating area of cliffs, beaches, salt marsh, mudflats and sandhills. Thousands of greylag and pink-footed geese overwinter here, and terns come to nest. The reserve also has the greatest concentration of eider ducks in Britain, while fulmars, kittiwakes and herring gulls live in the cliffs.

Footpaths from the car park on the reserve's western side lead for 3 miles east to the site of a lost village engulfed in 1413 by wind-blown sand. All that survives of the former settlement is the ruin of Forvie Kirk.

IONA St Columba called the 3½ mile long island 'Iona of my heart', and chose it as the site of his monastery. Nothing

remains of the original building of 563, thought to have been built of wattle and daub. In the Dark Ages the monastery was raided on several occasions by Vikings and its community massacred. Sixty Scottish kings were buried there, including Macbeth and Duncan, the 11th-century monarchs made famous by Shakespeare's tragedy *Macbeth*.

Iona's oldest building is St Oran's Chapel, built by Queen Margaret in 1080. The restored 13th-century abbey is the home of the Iona Community. Outside the abbey church is the beautifully carved St Martin's Cross, 5m (17ft) high and

FORVIE NATIONAL NATURE RESERVE ▶ 15 miles N of Aberdeen off A975.
IONA ▶ 1 mile off SW tip of Isle of Mull. Ferry all year from Fionnphort, Mull.

more than 1,000 years old. The 100m (328ft) hill of Dun I gives superb views to the Hebrides beyond. There is a ferry from Fionnphort, and day trips from Oban.

LOCH FYNE Measuring some 40 miles from its north-eastern tip to its mouth, Loch Fyne is one of Scotland's longest lochs. Its eastern shore provides dramatic views of forested ridges sweeping up from the water's edge.

In Cairndow, by the loch's head, the woodland gardens at Ardkinglass House are open throughout the year. South of the Heart of Argyll, a traditional gypsy wedding site, are the quiet villages of St Catherines and Strachur.

An exhilarating lochside road continues south past the ruined hulk of 15th-century Castle Lachlan, skirting the rocky shoreline to Otter Ferry. This village was named from the Gaelic word *oitir* for the great shingle bar that is exposed at low tide. At Kilfinan, a pre-Reformation church stands near the village's restored stagecoach inn.

From Millhouse, a small road heads west to Portavadie, an industrial 'ghost village' of the 1970s oil boom with a car ferry service to Tarbert. A picnic area just north of the village is the starting point for a hilly woodland trail.

LOCH FYNE ➡ A83 runs along north side of loch, A815 and B8000 run along south side.

Bow Fiddle Rock

MULL OF KINTYRE A steep and twisting 7-mile drive through spectacular hill scenery leads towards the peninsula's southwestern tip, though you have to walk the last few hundred yards to the lighthouse. The Antrim coast lies just 12 miles away, making this the closest point to Ireland on mainland Britain.

PORTKNOCKIE A quiet former fishing village, Portknockie sits on a cliff high above its harbour and is an excellent haven for small boats. From the cliff path to the east, strangely shaped rocks, including Bow Fiddle Rock, can be seen spearing out of the sea just offshore. Preacher's Cave, one of several caves along the rocky foreshore, was used as a church during the religious revival of the early 19th century. A 1½-mile clifftop walk west to Findochty offers superb views across the Moray Firth to the Black Isle.

ST CYRUS River banks, salt marshes, sand dunes, cliffs and a sandy beach make up one of Britain's most fascinating national nature reserves. The visitor centre illustrates the wonderful variety of birdlife, wild flowers and butterflies within the reserve. A short but steep path from the beach climbs to the village of St Cyrus, where a clifftop viewpoint looks out over the sea and to Montrose to the south. From the village an exhilarating path leads north to Woodston.

MULL OF KINTYRE ➡ 15 miles SW of Campbeltown.
PORTKNOCKIE ➡ 20 miles E of Elgin on A942.
ST CYRUS ➡ 5 miles N of Montrose off A92.

SCOTLAND

Fife & Southeast Scotland

ANSTRUTHER The harbour is home to the evocative Scottish Fisheries Museum although Anstruther's fishing fleet is now based at Pittenweem. Housed in 18th and 19th-century buildings that were once used as a chandlery and net loft, the museum depicts the lifestyle and history of a fishing community.

BASS ROCK The core of an ancient volcano poking up from the Firth of Forth, Bass Rock is a mile in circumference with almost perpendicular cliffs. Noted for its gannetry, the rock gave the gannet its scientific name, *Sula bassana*. Among the other seabirds you may see here are fulmars, cormorants, razorbills and puffins. Additional attractions are a lighthouse, the ruins of a 16th-century chapel and the remains of a fort that was used as a state prison from 1671 to 1701. Boat trips around the rock start from North Berwick.

THE BINNS In 1944, the spacious 17th-century house was the first country mansion taken over by the National Trust for Scotland. Its name comes from the Gaelic *beinn*, meaning

ANSTRUTHER ➡ 9 miles S of St Andrews.
BASS ROCK ➡ Off North Berwick, 22 miles NE of Edinburgh.
THE BINNS ➡ 5 miles W of Queensferry on A904.

'mountain', although the house stands on only a modest slope. This is the ancestral home of the Dalyell family, whose most noted member was Thomas or Tam. A royalist during the Civil War, he became a commander in the Russian Tsarist army and, finally, was a scourge of the Presbyterian Covenanters back in Scotland. In 1681, he founded the Royal Scots Greys regiment at The Binns, which has many mementos of him.

The house is noted for its moulded plaster ceilings in four of the rooms. A short woodland walk leads you northeast to the panoramic Tower Viewpoint, which looks out over the Forth and the surrounding hills.

COLDINGHAM White-capped breakers roll in and beach huts line the dunes at Coldingham Sands. The priory

at Coldingham is one of the glories of this part of Scotland. Now used as a parish church, it evolved from the restored choir of a ruined medieval priory, most of which was demolished by Cromwell's cannons in 1648. The most notable interior feature of the building is the delicate arching and arcading of the north and east walls. In happier times, a thousand retainers of Mary, Queen of Scots, were accommodated in the priory during her 1566 progress through the Borders.

South of the village, the Coldingham to Eyemouth coast path winds through steep grassy hills, while smaller tracks circle and zigzag around them.

COLDINGHAM ➥ Need 3 miles NW of Eyemouth on A1107.

CRAIL From the tolbooth and the market cross to the pretty harbour area, the townscape of this little burgh remains unspoiled, conserved by individual property owners and the National Trust for Scotland. The museum and heritage centre tells the story of Crail's involvement with royalty, fishing, golf and the air station on the road to Fife Ness.

The parapet Castle Walk, which follows the remains of a castle wall along a cliff path, gives views of the harbour and, on a clear day, St Abb's Head, 30 miles to the south, can be seen. Crail has two well-known golf courses, the Balcomie and Craighead Links.

CULROSS Red-tiled roofs, crow-stepped gables and cobbled streets, all beautifully restored, recall the heyday of Culross (pronounced 'Cooross') in the 16th and 17th centuries, when it was Scotland's wealthiest town. Salt and coal exports made a fortune for Sir George Bruce, an early 17th-century laird of Culross. Bruce's mansion, completed in 1611, was so grand that it became known as The Palace. Here you can see rare wall and ceiling paintings and a massive strong-room. In 1932, it was bought by the National Trust for Scotland, at a cost of £700.

Sir George Bruce and his family are buried in partly restored Culross Abbey, now the parish church. Many of the gravestones here bear the royal warrant symbol of the

CRAIL ➡ 12 miles SE of St Andrews on A917.
CULROSS ➡ 5 miles E of Kincardine off A985.

Culross Hammermen, who for generations until the mid 18th century held the monopoly on making all of Scotland's iron-baking 'girdles', or griddles.

Much conservation work has been carried out in the burgh. The NTS visitor centre, with an exhibition and video presentation outlining Culross's history, is located in the Town House. The House with the Evil Eyes takes its name from the design of a window high on its Dutch gable. Another restored house conceals an electricity substation.

HOPETOUN HOUSE The seat of the Marquess of Linlithgow, this elegant stately home still contains many

of its 18th-century furnishings, tapestries, portraits and porcelain. The original house, built by Sir William Bruce, was later enlarged and extensively modified by William Adam and his sons, and finally completed in 1702. Several separate exhibtions are housed here.

The grounds include walks through woodland, nature trails and a spacious park where you can see red deer and Hebridean sheep. On the edge of the grounds, Abercorn Church dates partly from the 12th century, although some of its masonry came from the 7th-century monastery of Abercurnig. This once occupied the same site when the area was part of the kingdom of Northumbria.

HOPETOUN HOUSE ■▶ 3 miles W of Queensferry N of A904.

INCHCOLM ISLAND The ruins of 12th-century St Colm's Abbey stand on Inchcolm Island in the Firth of Forth, reached by a summer ferry service from North Queensferry. Seals, seagulls and puffins are the island's only inhabitants today, but old tunnels and gun emplacements are a reminder of its sterner wartime role. Back on the mainland, a heritage trail in South Queensferry takes in places of interest, including inns, a hexagonal Signal House and a remarkable number of wells.

ST ABBS Rows of neat cottages overlook the harbour of the fishing village, which takes its name from a Northumbrian princess who became the abbess of a nearby nunnery in the 7th century. On St Abb's Head to the north, kittiwakes and guillemots, herring gulls, fulmars and puffins throng the cliffs and rock stacks of a national nature reserve (NTS). From the visitor centre, there are footpaths and a road to the large natural amphitheatre of Pettico Wick. The sheep-cropped grassland leading towards Harelaw Hill offers wide views to the Cheviots and the Lomond hills of Fife. Swans, grebes and tufted ducks are attracted to the reedy Mire Loch, in a low-lying geological fault, while Scotland's only voluntary marine reserve lies offshore. Run by local people, its aim is to conserve the marine environment and increase public awareness; wardens conduct 'rock-pool rambles' in summer, describing the wildlife found there. On the cliffs to the northwest are the ruins of Fast Castle.

INCHCOLM ISLAND ➡ Boats from South Queensferry, E of Forth Road Bridge.
ST ABBS ➡ 15 miles N of Berwick-upon-Tweed on B6438 off A1 Dunbar road.

ST ANDREWS Named after Scotland's patron saint, St Andrews is internationally recognised as the home of golf, and today has the British Golf Museum and no fewer than six golf courses. The Old Course is on the northern edge of the town, in full view of several streets; a right of way called Grannie Clark's Wynd crosses the 1st and 18th fairways.

Running parallel to the Old Course is West Sands, one of the town's two extensive beaches, while East Sands stretches beyond the rivermouth harbour, which shelters lobster boats.

South Street, entered through a 16th-century gateway, has narrow alleys known as 'rigs' branching off it. The street leads to the ruin of 12th-century St Andrews Cathedral (HS), where you can climb the tower for a fine view across the city.

Other attractions include the university (founded in 1410 and the third oldest in Britain), the Victorian Botanic Garden and St Andrews Castle (HS), built around 1200, with a forbidding dungeon. Two miles inland, Craigtoun Country Park features a Dutch-style model village, built on a lake island.

ST ANDREWS ▶▶ 12 miles SE of Dundee on A91.

SCOTLAND
North Highlands & Islands

APPLECROSS The little village of Applecross is set on a sheltered bay, with wooded hills behind that make it a haven in a bleak environment. The road east out of the village climbs into the lunar landscape of the 610m (2,000ft) high Bealach na Bà, or Pass of the Cattle, where there can be blizzards even in midsummer. Following the hairpin bends that twist down to Loch Kishorn can be a memorable and challenging experience.

The route that hugs the coast from Applecross to Shieldaig passes scattered crofts that were extraordinarily remote until the road was built in the 1970s. Closer to Shieldaig, it offers splendid views across Loch Torridon to the Torridon Mountains – among the most ancient in the world, composed of sandstone that is more than 600 million years old.

ARDNAMURCHAN The tip of this long peninsula, the Point of Ardnamurchan, is the most westerly part of mainland Britain, where local time, according to the sun, is 30 minutes behind Greenwich Mean Time. From Salen, the road along the peninsula passes through lush woods and rhododendron

APPLECROSS ➡➡ Along minor roads off A896, N of Kyle of Lochalsh.
ARDNAMURCHAN ➡➡ 80 miles W of Fort William at end of B8007, off A861.

thickets beside Loch Sunart before crossing desolate moors round Ben Hiant, the core of an extinct volcano. The Natural History Centre at Glenmore has displays relating to local wildlife. From the scattered village of Kilchoan a car ferry operates to Tobermory on the Isle of Mull.

A lighthouse stands on the clifftop at the Point of Ardnamurchan. Sanna Bay, to the northeast, has a sandy beach sheltered from the winds by dunes covered by machair grass. Kilmory, on the peninsula's wild, isolated northern coast, has an ancient burial ground and sandy beaches flanked by caves.

BALINTORE In Balintore's harbour, local boat owners provide fishing and seabird viewing trips, while to the northeast, at Hilton of Cadboll, are the remains of the ancient Our Lady's Chapel (HS). The Pictish stone that originally stood next to the chapel is now in the Royal Museum of Scotland in Edinburgh.

South of Shandwick, a seaside village that merges into Balintore, stands the magnificent Clach a' Charridh, a tall Pictish cross-slab, carved with abstract patterns and figures of angels, huntsmen, warriors and animals.

BALINTORE ➨ 8 miles SE of Tain at end of B9166.

BARRA The strange charm of Barra immediately strikes visitors who fly here and land, tides permitting, not on a runway but on an immense beach of firm white sand. The 14-mile road encircling much of this strikingly beautiful island makes it easy to explore. Several side roads wander off to the bays and beaches or into green glens beneath the central hills.

The main town and ferry port of Castlebay in the south is dominated by Kisimul Castle, which rises straight out of the waters of the bay. This is the home of the MacNeil of Barra, whose forebears were the terror of the western seas for hundreds of years until the 16th century. When they had dined, a bard would announce from the battlements, 'The MacNeil has supped; now the princes of the world may sit down to eat.' There are guided tours of the castle in summer.

At Cille-bharra, the 12th-century Church of St Barr has a replica of a unique grave slab featuring both Norse runic markings and a Celtic cross. The writer Sir Compton Mackenzie is buried there. On the slopes of Heaval is a statue of the Madonna and Child, a reminder that Barra's inhabitants are mostly Catholic. The site has spectacular views to the islands of Vatersay, Sandray, Pabbay, Mingulay and Berneray.

With a healthy income derived from tourism, fishing and seafood-processing, Barra is one of the most prosperous communities in the Western Isles. Perfume is also made on the island, and shell grit is supplied for masonry paint. A children's festival is held here every July.

BARRA ➡ Ferries from Oban on mainland and Lochboisdale on South Uist.

One of the most prosperous communities in the Western Isles

BROUGH OF BIRSAY In spring Orkney's Brough of Birsay (HS) is aglow with sea pinks. Reached by a causeway at low tide, it offers many historical remains, including Pictish and Viking farmsteads, and a 12th-century Romanesque church, while the 16th-century Earl's Palace (HS) in Birsay village was built in Renaissance style. Birsay Moors and Marwick Head are two of several RSPB reserves on Mainland.

BUTT OF LEWIS The northern tip of the Isle of Lewis is a windswept spot, exposed to the unleashed power of the waves. In Eoropaidh, the island's northernmost village, is the 12th-century St Moluag's Chapel. From nearby Port of Ness, the men of the parish sail each September to the island of Sulisgeir to harvest the young 'gugas', or gannets, which are a local delicacy. In the village of Siadar are the ruins of Teampull Pheadair, a 12th-century chapel, the Steinacleit stone circle and the vast monolith of Clach an Trushal. Some 45 miles north of the Butt of Lewis, the island of North Rona is a nature reserve – and some 200 miles beyond lie the Faeroes.

CALANAIS STANDING STONES In the majesty of their setting – and their inscrutability – the standing stones outside the hamlet of Calanais on Lewis rival those of Stonehenge and Carnac. Located some 6m (20ft) high on a

BROUGH OF BIRSAY ➡ 20 miles NW of Kirkwall on A966, Orkney Islands.
BUTT OF LEWIS ➡ 22 miles N of Stornoway on A857, Isle of Lewis.
CALANAIS STANDING STONES ➡ 12 miles W of Stornoway off A858.

hill above East Loch Roag, the Calanais Standing Stones (HS) were quarried locally and erected about 4,000 years ago in roughly the form of a Celtic cross, with a chambered cairn in the centre. Their meaning will probably never be known, but they appear to have astronomical significance and they align with other standing stones and circles in the area.

South of Calanais, the B8011 runs through rugged, near-deserted terrain. Where the road bends sharply round the tip of narrow Little Loch Roag, a rough and often muddy 2½-mile path leads to the remains of a group of curious 'beehive' dwellings – a rare example of a primitive Hebridean form of housing in which stones were positioned to form a hollow hillock about 1.8m (6ft) high. Farther on is the sandy beach of Uig Sands, where in 1831 a set of Norse chess pieces – the Lewis Chessmen – was discovered in the dunes.

CAPE WRATH A lighthouse, built in 1828, crowns the windswept, wave-battered northwestern tip of mainland Scotland. To the east, the highest cliffs on the British mainland rise to 280m (920ft) at Clò Mor. Cape Wrath can be reached by a passenger ferry across the Kyle of Durness, then a track crossing The Parbh, a huge wilderness. In summer, a minibus takes visitors along the 10-mile route. The cliffs and track lie within a Ministry of Defence bombing range, and walkers should check on restrictions.

CAPE WRATH ▶ 10 miles NW of Durness.

CARLOWAY BROCH

CARLOWAY BROCH **The Iron Age broch, or fortified tower, standing on a crag** by the hamlet of Dun Charlabhaigh on Lewis is a testament to the skills of its masons. Some 2,000 years after they were erected, the dry-stone walls are still 9m (30ft) high in some places. The central courtyard is 8m (25ft) across and surrounded by double walls containing galleries, chambers and flights of stairs. In the nearby village of Garenin, you can visit a group of traditional thatched 'blackhouses', one of which is now a renovated hostel.

CASTLE TIORAM

CASTLE TIORAM **A sandspit, occasionally covered by high water, connects the romantically sited island fortress** of Castle Tioram with the wooded shores of Loch Moidart. The castle is said to have been built in 1353, although the curtain wall is probably far older. For centuries, it was the home of the chieftains of Clanranald. In 1715, it was deliberately burnt down when Allan Clanranald, the 14th chieftain, departed to fight beside James Edward Stuart, the Old Pretender. He was convinced – rightly, as it turned out – that he would not return alive.

The Silver Walk, where buried treasure was once found, leads along the cliffs of Loch Moidart and then inland to the abandoned settlement of Port a' Bhàta, whose inhabitants were transported to Australia in 1853 during the final stages of the Highland Clearances.

CARLOWAY BROCH ➡ 6 miles N of Calanais on A858, Isle of Lewis.
CASTLE TIORAM ➡ 36 miles S of Mallaig off A861.

DUART CASTLE Of all the fortresses in the Western Isles, none is more expressive of the power and majesty of medieval chieftains than Duart Castle on the Isle of Mull. The forbidding clifftop building dates from the 13th century, with additions made towards the end of the 14th century by the Macleans. In 1912, the castle was restored from a ruinous state to its former grandeur and to its position as rallying place of the Clan Maclean. Inside are a collection of family relics, an exhibition on chiefs of the clan and a Scouting exhibition; the 27th clan chief was for many years leader of the Scout movement in the Commonwealth. The views from the Sea Room are especially breathtaking.

DUNCANSBY HEAD A lighthouse on the headland guards the entrance to the Pentland Firth. A path from the car park descends to a shingle beach, giving superb views of the chasms, arches and stacks carved out of the sandstone cliffs. At low tide you can walk through a natural doorway in the rock towards Duncansby Stacks, remnants of an ancient cliff line eroded by the sea and rowdy with gannets, fulmars, skuas, guillemots and puffins.

DUNNET BAY Standing on Dunnet Head, more than 91m (300ft) above the sea at the bay's northern end, you have the feeling of being at the edge of the world. It is certainly

DUART CASTLE ➡ 22 miles SE of Tobermory, Isle of Mull.
DUNCANSBY HEAD ➡ 1 mile E of John O'Groats.
DUNNET BAY ➡ 6 miles E of Thurso on A836.

one of Britain's remotest edges – the mainland's most northerly point. Dunnet Head and its lighthouse are reached by a road which winds over the high moors from the village of Dunnet.

South of the head, Dunnet Bay has a long sandy beach, where you will find a natural history visitor centre. Ranger-guided walks start at the centre and lead through a nearby forest, home to several species of butterfly. The walk continues through Dunnet Links National Nature Reserve, where terns, gannets and auks can be seen. In Dunnet village, Mary-Ann's Cottage, named after a former occupant, shows life on an early croft and is open to the public.

DUNROBIN CASTLE The castle and its luxuriant formal gardens command far-ranging views.

Since the 13th century, Dunrobin Castle has been in the hands of the Earls and Dukes of Sutherland, whose family played a leading role in the Highland Clearances. Its original massive keep has been embellished with turrets and pinnacles, first in the 19th century by Sir Charles Barry, architect of the Houses of Parliament in London, then by Sir Robert Lorimer after a fire in 1915. The castle museum contains Pictish stones and a number of mementos of the Victorian era.

DUNROBIN CASTLE ➡ 2 miles N of Golspie on A9.

EIGG In the north of the island, the Singing Sands (Camas Sgiotaig) squeak when walked upon, or even emit a long, continuous moan when the wind is in the right direction. Together with the neighbouring islands of Rùm, Canna and Muck, Eigg forms the Small Islands Parish of the Church of Scotland, and with its population of about 70 it is the most crowded of the four. There are sandy beaches to the south of the Singing Sands and to the north of Galmisdale. For visitors interested in geology there are fine walks round the cliffs of An Sgurr, and bicycles, mopeds, ponies and dinghies may be hired.

EIGG ➡ Ferry from Mallaig.

EILEAN DONAN CASTLE

EILEAN DONAN CASTLE The battlements and turrets of a romantic castle rise from a rocky islet at the meeting place of three lochs. Eilean Donan was built in the 13th century as a Highland stronghold of the Scottish kings, and was later held by the MacKenzies and their loyal followers, the Macraes. After centuries of turbulent clan warfare, the castle was finally destroyed by British forces during the abortive Jacobite uprising in 1719. The ruins were fully restored between 1911 and 1932, and you can see Macrae portraits and furniture.

EILEAN DONAN CASTLE ➡ 10 miles E of Kyle of Lochalsh on A87.

Eilean Donan Castle

INVEREWE GARDEN In 1862, Osgood Mackenzie inherited the Inverewe estate, then a barren wilderness,

and turned it into a subtropical Eden. Taking advantage of the North Atlantic Drift which gives the northwest coast of Scotland its mild, humid weather, Mackenzie planted trees as shelter belts against the prevailing winds, improved the soil, and over the next 60 years created an internationally renowned environment in which subtropical plants could flourish.

Inverewe Garden (NTS) is criss-crossed by a maze of paths that meander through woodland, shrubberies and water gardens. The gardens are most colourful in spring and early summer when the rhododendrons and azaleas are in flower, but autumn brings an equally dazzling display.

JARLSHOF Grassy mounds along with the remains of walls, doors, hearths and passageways mark one

of Britain's most remarkable archaeological sites. An interpretation centre shows finds excavated at Jarlshof – the relics of 3,000 years of human settlement, from the Stone Age through the Bronze and Iron Ages to Viking times.

From here, take the road south to Sumburgh Head, the southern tip of Shetland's Mainland, capped by a lighthouse. The area is part of an RSPB nature reserve, where seabirds roost by the thousand and seals clamber on and off the rocks along the seashore.

INVEREWE GARDEN ▶➔ 6 miles NE of Gairloch on A832.
JARLSHOF ▶➔ 22 miles S of Lerwick, Shetland Islands.

KNOYDART The Knoydart peninsula, between Loch Hourn and Loch Nevis, remains an utterly remote area of unspoilt wilderness. Inverie has a shop, a school, a restaurant and a pub, even a small library – but no road to connect it to the rest of the world. Day trips or longer visits must be made by boat from Mallaig. Quite unlike the landscape of Loch Hourn, the shoreline of Loch Nevis is an open and bright place, a paradise for walkers and escapists.

MEY The rocks called the Men of Mey, off St John's Point, present a fearsome sight when the ebb tide throws huge gouts of roaring water 9 to 12m (30 to 40ft) high and blows spume far inland. Nearby stands the Castle of Mey, built on the site of a stronghold of the Sinclairs in the 16th century. In 1952, the castle became a summer residence of the late Queen Elizabeth, the Queen Mother, and the castle and gardens are now open in summer. In the village of Mey, the Castle Arms Hotel has photographs of the Royal Family taken during visits to Caithness.

East of Mey, at Kirkstyle, is the Old Canisbay Kirk of St Drostan, whose oldest parts date from the 15th century. In the porch is a grave slab dedicated to the memory of members of the de Groot, or Groat, family who gave their name to the settlement of John O' Groats, 2½ miles to the east.

KNOYDART ➡ NE of Mallaig.
MEY ➡ 15 miles NE of Thurso on A836.

MOUSA BROCH The most complete example of an Iron Age broch (dry-stone tower)

can be found on this small uninhabited island, reached by boat from Sandwick. The tower rises 13m (43ft) with walls that are 4m (12ft) thick at the base. Inside, a clan of Picts constructed a 'wheelhouse' of thatched wooden rooms set in a circle.

OLD MAN OF HOY Towering sandstone cliffs and a 137m (450ft) sea stack,

known as the Old Man of Hoy, greet travellers passing the island of Hoy by ferry from Scrabster. Reached by a 2-mile footpath from Rackwick, the stack is within the North Hoy RSPB Reserve, where rare red-throated divers can be seen in summer. Hoy is also distinctive for its myriad wild flowers that grow at low altitudes. The Dwarfie Stane (HS), a tomb carved from a sandstone block around 3000 BC, stands beside the road to Rackwick.

PLOCKTON Palm trees line the waterfront of this delightful village,

a favoured haunt of artists, naturalists and sailors. You can hire small boats or take a trip to see the seal colonies on islands round the rocky headland. Pine martens and golden eagles are sometimes spotted in the woods and hills to the south of Plockton, and to the east Craig Highland Farm has rare breeds of domestic animals.

MOUSA BROCH ⏵ By boat from Sandwick on Shetland Islands, 14 miles S of Lerwick.
OLD MAN OF HOY ⏵ 7 miles SW of Linksness on Hoy, Orkney Islands.
PLOCKTON ⏵ 5 miles NE of Kyle of Lochalsh on minor roads.

RÙM Wild and mountainous, the island rises steeply from the sea to peaks of 700m (2,300ft) and more. Few people have lived there since 1826, when almost the entire population was shipped across the Atlantic to Newfoundland in Canada.

In 1957, Rùm became a national nature reserve. Two signposted nature trails start from the dock, near the head of Loch Scresort. One follows the loch's southern shore, part of which is frequented by otters, and ends 1½ miles away at Port nan Caranean, an abandoned village where eider ducks and gulls nest among the ruins. The other trail heads inland for about 2 miles.

Red deer are everywhere. There are also wild goats and little Rùm ponies bred on the island to carry deer carcasses down from the hills. You may also spot golden eagles and, more rarely, sea eagles. The latter, which has a wingspan of 2.7m (9ft), became extinct in Britain early in the 20th century but was reintroduced to Rùm in the 1970s. Grey and common seals hunt for fish in the offshore waters, and in the long summer evenings Manx shearwaters gather on the waves by the thousand, before returning to their mountaintop nests, where they rear their young in burrows.

SKARA BRAE For centuries the 4,500-year-old village of Skara Brae (HS) was buried beneath dunes until it re-emerged during a storm in 1850. Sand had preserved the walls of stone houses and their domestic furniture, including

RÙM ➡ Ferry from Mallaig.
SKARA BRAE ➡ 18 miles W of Kirkwall, Orkney Islands.

food boxes lined with clay to act as refrigerators. There are even what appear to have been lavatories. The village was home to people whose way of life was more sophisticated than that of many 19th-century crofters.

SMOO CAVE A curving flight of steps, followed by stepping stones, leads down to the vast Smoo Cave,
whose name derives from the Norse word *smjuga*, meaning 'narrow cleft'. A wooden walkway extends into a second chamber, where the Allt Smoo burn falls 24m (80ft) from an opening in the roof. A third chamber is practically inaccessible by foot, but can be visited by boat trips in summer.

STAFFA Resembling a cathedral, with its huge walls formed from hexagonal basalt columns,
Fingal's Cave on the isle of Staffa provided the inspiration for Mendelssohn's overture *The Hebrides*. In the first half of the 19th century, the lonely grandeur of the tiny uninhabited island attracted visitors such as Tennyson, Turner, Wordsworth and Queen Victoria. Legend has it that the giant Torquil MacLeod was building the Giant's Causeway in Ireland and took home a sackful of his work, but the sack burst and the rocks were scattered, the largest being Staffa. You can reach the island by boat from Fionnphort, the Isle of Ulva and Oban.

SMOO CAVE ➡ 2 miles SE of Durness on A838.
STAFFA ➡ W of Isle of Mull.

STONES OF STENNESS Standing on the southern edge of the Loch of Harray on Orkney's Mainland, the

Stones of Stenness (HS) are a 3rd-century BC stone circle of which only four monoliths survive. The nearby Ring of Brogar (HS) is a wider circle of 27 stones.

Orkney's largest freshwater loch, Loch of Harray offers plentiful fishing for brown trout. To the southeast is Maes Howe (HS), a huge cairn with the world's largest collection of runic inscriptions in one place. Corrigall Farm Museum, off the A986, re-creates an 18th-century farmstead.

TOBERMORY The main town of Mull is a place of colour-washed houses and hotels, with shops selling items

such as ship chandlery, fishing tackle, diving gear and guns. Tobermory was built in the 1780s, when the British Society for Encouraging Fisheries decided to establish a port on this fine natural harbour on Mull's northeastern coast. Fishing boats are now joined by pleasure craft and boats offering visitors trips for skate and mackerel. Except in midwinter, a ferry runs between Tobermory and Kilchoan, on the mainland peninsula of Ardnamurchan to the north.

In Aros Park, a 10-minute walk from the town centre, woodland walks lead past rhododendrons and waterfalls. On its edge, at Druimfin, the Mull Little Theatre has established a new production centre.

STONES OF STENNESS ➡ 10 miles W of Kirkwall on A965, Orkney Islands.
TOBERMORY ➡ Isle of Mull, ferry from Oban.

SCOTLAND
Southwest Scotland

AILSA CRAIG Ten miles offshore, the 335m (1,100ft) high plug of a long-extinct volcano dominates the view from most of the coastline. The island is home to guillemots, kittiwakes and thousands of gannets, which breed here every summer. Former tenants of the island used to pay their rents in gannet feathers. Ailsa granite was long used to make what were regarded as the finest stones for use in the sport of curling.

CAERLAVEROCK NATURE RESERVE Barnacle geese from Spitsbergen come to spend autumn and winter on the nature reserve at the Caerlaverock Wetland Centre, along with pink-footed geese from Iceland and other wildfowl. There is also a large colony of rare natterjack toads. At East Park Farm, viewing towers and hides are open to the public all year round, and between May and August you can take guided walks.

On the edge of the reserve, the deep red sandstone ruins of Caerlaverock Castle (HS) are reflected in its moat. Built in the late 13th century overlooking the Merse saltings, the castle changed hands several times between the English and the Scots. One of its most remarkable features is a 17th-century row of interconnecting buildings that looks more like a Renaissance mansion than part of a fortress.

AILSA CRAIG ➡ Off coast at Girvan.
CAERLAVEROCK NATURE RESERVE ➡ 8 miles SE of Dumfries on B725.

CAIRN HOLY The chambered cairns of Cairn Holy (HS) date from 4,000–5,000 years ago. The larger of the two has an exposed burial chamber as well as a small courtyard in which ritual ceremonies took place. The smaller cairn was robbed for building stones in the 18th century.

CORSEWALL POINT At the northwestern tip of a windswept almost treeless peninsula, deep-cut rock fissures bring the waves battering upwards into plumes of spray. On the headland above stands the white tower of Corsewall Lighthouse, completed in 1816. Now a hotel, it was designed by Robert Stevenson, grandfather of the writer Robert Louis Stevenson.

CULZEAN CASTLE Until the mid 18th century Culzean (pronounced 'Cullain') was a simple medieval tower house perched on a cliff edge. Then, in 1777, the 10th Earl of Cassillis engaged Robert Adam to transform the building. The finest features of Culzean Castle (NTS) include an oval staircase and the round drawing room with views over the Firth of Clyde. A flat at the top of the castle was given to General Eisenhower in recognition of his achievements during the Second World War; he stayed there four times, and an exhibition covers his time in Britain. A visitor centre in Adam's Home Farm is the focal point of a country park with a swan pond and walled garden.

SCOTLAND Southwest Scotland

CAIRN HOLY ➡ 6 miles W of Gatehouse of Fleet off A75.
CORSEWALL POINT ➡ 10 miles N of Stranraer.
CULZEAN CASTLE ➡ 12 miles S of Ayr on A719.

ISLE OF WHITHORN

ISLE OF WHITHORN A causeway leads to the rocky peninsula that gave the village its name. Once a genuine isle, the headland has the ruined 13th-century St Ninian's Chapel, named after the saint said to have converted the southern Scots to Christianity in the 5th century. In the Middle Ages, Ninian's shrine in the town of Whithorn, 4 miles inland, was one of Scotland's major pilgrimage centres. The Whithorn Museum (HS) displays archaeological finds associated with the saint.

KIRKCUDBRIGHT

KIRKCUDBRIGHT In the early 20th century, artists and fishermen congregated in Kirkcudbright (pronounced 'Kirkoobree'). For a flavour of those times, visit Broughton House (NTS), bequeathed to the town by the painter E.A. Hornel (1864–1933), which has a collection of his paintings and sculptures. Near the harbour, MacLellan's Castle (HS) is a ruined 16th-century mansion, while the medieval Tolbooth in the largely Georgian high street now houses crafts studios and exhibitions of the works of contemporary artists.

LOGAN BOTANIC GARDEN

LOGAN BOTANIC GARDEN An exotic walled garden has been arranged round the ruined keep of Castle Balzieland. The warming effect of the Gulf Stream enables eucalyptus, cabbage palms, tree ferns and other plants native to the Southern Hemisphere to grow here.

ISLE OF WHITHORN ➡ 4 miles SE of Whithorn on B7004.
KIRKCUDBRIGHT ➡ 36 miles SW of Dumfries off A75.
LOGAN BOTANIC GARDEN ➡ 14 miles S of Stranraer off A716.

Index

Picture Credits

Acknowledgements

For Toucan Books
Editors Jane Hutchings,
Andrew Kerr-Jarrett
Art Editor Nick Avery
Picture Research Sharon Southren,
Mia Stewart-Wilson, Christine Vincent
Proofreader Marion Dent
Indexer Michael Dent

For Reader's Digest Books
Editorial Director Julian Browne
Art Director Anne-Marie Bulat
Managing Editor Nina Hathway
Project Editor Rachel Weaver
Project Art Editor Julie Bennett
Picture Resource Manager
Sarah Stewart-Richardson
Pre-press Technical Manager
Dean Russell
Senior Production Controller
Katherine Tibbals

Origination by ImageScanhouse

Printed and bound in China

Front cover Devon coast. **Back cover** Clovelly, Devon. **Page 1** Whitby, Yorkshire. **Pages 2–3** Lizard, Cornwall. **Pages 4–5** Wells-next-the-Sea, Norfolk. **Page 6** Blakeney Point, Norfolk. **Pages 8–9** Near Tintagel, Cornwall. **Pages 44–45** White Cliffs of Dover, Kent. **Pages 68–69** Burnham Overy, Norfolk. **Pages 88–89** North Pier, Blackpool. **Pages 102–103** Bamburgh Castle, Northumberland. **Pages 118–119** Whitesands Beach, St David's. **Pages 144–145** Isle of Skye, Scotland.

The Most Amazing Places on Britain's Coast is based on material from **Reader's Digest Illustrated Guide to Britain's Coast**, published by The Reader's Digest Association Limited, London

Copyright © 2010 The Reader's Digest Association Limited,
11 Westferry Circus, Canary Wharf,
London E14 4HE
www.readersdigest.co.uk

We are committed both to the quality of our products and the service we provide to our customers. We value your comments, so please do contact us on **08705 113366** or via our website at **www.readersdigest.co.uk**

If you have any comments or suggestions about the contents of our books, email us at **gbeditorial@readersdigest.co.uk**

ISBN 978 0276 44573 6
Book Code 400-478 UP0000-1
Oracle Code 250014573S.00.24